# Lose the Debate

A Practical Guide to Emotional
Intelligence and Successful Dialogue

DR. SUMMER ALLEN

Summer Allen
**Lose the Debate**

ISBN:
Paperback: 9798872564348
Hardcover: 9798862018028

Copyright © 2023

*Sometimes when we lose, we actually win.*
**—Dr. Summer Allen**

# Lose
# the
# Debate

# Table of Contents

# Introduction

*"Why does everything have to be about race?"*

*"Guns don't kill people. People kill people."*

*"I think all lives matter—not just black lives.
Saying that isn't fair to everyone else."*

*"I'm not going to call a person 'them.' That's not
even grammatically correct. People just need to live
based on the gender they were born with."*

*"Global warming isn't real."*

*"Hiring people based on diversity lowers the bar."*

Wow! Those are some powerful statements. Whether we agree with them or not, they are related to some of today's most significant societal topics. How often have you gotten into an uncomfortable conversation that started with statements like these over the past few years? These are the types of conversations that, thirty seconds in, create an awkward visceral response.

Your body tenses up, you feel a knot in your stomach and a lump in your throat. Your anxiety builds, and everything from your conversation partner's perspective to their tone makes you boil. At that moment, you discover that your opinions are vastly different. You cannot understand how they can think the way they do. As your anxiety continues to rise, you are afraid that anything you say will transform a friendly dialogue into a full-blown argument. Some of us take an avoidant approach where we either end the conversation or get to a point where we wish for something—anything—to end the conversation in its tracks. It could be a phone ringing or an extinction-level asteroid strike; it doesn't matter as long as you don't have to utter another word about this topic. On the other hand, some of us get a rush of emotion and feel a sense of obligation to tackle this topic head-on and change the other person's "twisted" views of the topic in an attempt to save them from themselves and make the world a better place. While both scenarios may seem a bit dramatic, the truth is these types of conversations happen every day, whether they are planned discussions or come out of nowhere.

While most of our conversations are not about major world issues, that doesn't mean that even our everyday conversations are easy. Discovering that we have divergent opinions and perspectives from someone we interact with regularly is challenging. These difficult conversations are part of life—like talking with your siblings about how to best care for an aging parent, setting boundaries with a friend who doesn't respect your time, or providing an employee constructive feedback on their work products. It could look like conversing with your ex-spouse about disciplining your child or telling a partner you want a divorce. These are just a few tough conversations that are often difficult to navigate.

I wish that the contents of this book could make tough conversations simpler, but the truth is difficult conversations are always going to be difficult. I can promise you that I've made a career out of studying how people interact and communicate. As a result, I have developed strategies that will help you to navigate through and benefit from even the most uncomfortable talks. This book will provide practical tools and methods to enable you and your conversation partner to leave a tough conversation feeling whole and understood.

As the owner of a leadership development firm, my business is built on difficult conversations. Every day, I work to bring out commonalities while enabling people to appreciate the unique differences that we all have. This ranges from our individual identities and our unique life experiences to our diverse perspectives. I've identified that much of the divisiveness happening in our world is due to a lack of open dialogue and willingness to have courageous conversations in order to better understand one another and reach a solution.

I began to dig into how to tackle difficult conversations while receiving my doctorate from the University of Southern California; my dissertation was titled *The Moderating Effects of Leader Behavior on Employee Turnover.* The paper aimed to understand top leaders' behaviors that drove employees to make one of the most significant decisions of their lives—to quit their jobs. We have all heard the quote, "People don't leave jobs. They leave their leaders." My research validated that claim. A leader's lack of emotional intelligence (EI) is the number one leadership behavior that drives employees to quit. Though I specialize in leadership development, my niche is EI. My dissertation's approach was to take the leaders step-by-step through this challenging process.

Before we go further, let's understand what EI means. EI is one's ability to effectively acknowledge, identify, and communicate their emotions as well as understand the emotions of others. After starting my leadership development practice, I realized emotional intelligence is not just a challenge in leadership that impacted behaviors and relationships—it is a challenge for everyone. EI is a key component to having courageous conversations. It has been the driving force behind my work ever since.

One of the main components of EI is self-awareness: having a deep understanding of self, who you are, and why you are the way you are. When working with leaders to enhance their leadership performance through EI, I first help leaders understand the importance of acknowledging their past experiences and how those experiences shape who they are as a person and a leader. To have true self-awareness, we must understand how our past experiences, or historical context, influence and shape our present perspective. Once our historical context has been explored and mapped out, I challenge leaders to recognize how those experiences influence how they show up, make decisions, and connect with people. The same level of self-awareness is required in a courageous conversation.

## The Power of Perspective

Our perspective is powerful. It is how we define the world. It is the lens through which we see the world, and it dictates how we show up in it. Our perspective is our mental blueprint. However, we often neglect to reflect or deeply understand our perspective. We form our perspective based on our individual life experiences. What was your family like growing up? Who did you grow up around? Who didn't you grow up around? Where did you live when you were younger? What religion were your parents, and did they pass those traditions on to you? Did you experience any childhood traumas? Everything you experienced from birth until now has developed the road map that is your perspective. Your perspective defines how you see the world. How you see the world then drives your behaviors, opinions, and views. It influences what you gravitate to and what you avoid, your likes and dislikes, your parenting style, your value system, whom you choose to date, your communication style, and much more. Neglecting to understand how our perspective is formed and how it influences our current behaviors limits our ability to understand ourselves and grow.

The truth is we are never without influence from our historical context. Even as an adult, parent, or leader in a workplace, you are still influenced by your parents, childhood neighborhood, and even the playground bully from third grade. Once you intentionally reflect on your historical context and understand the significant impact specific experiences have on your subconscious, you can understand yourself better, keep what serves you, and remove thoughts and perspectives that hinder growth. When you are more self-aware, you can perform at a higher leadership and interpersonal capacity, communicate more effectively, and engage and lead more successfully in diverse cultures.

I see breakthroughs in self-awareness in almost every one of my seminars. In one class, I took a senior executive through a self-awareness exercise. The executive grew up in a strict religious family and community. After the training, he realized that being taught certain ideals by his parents created stereotypes, biases, and judgments that did not lend themselves to a mindset of inclusion. He could see that this mindset kept him from authentically connecting with specific team and organization members. This story is just one of many examples of how your past experiences influence how you see the world and connect with others. However, these experiences are often pushed into our subconscious, never to be unpacked and understood. Ultimately, you move into a leadership position or a team environment unaware of how your past influences every aspect of your professional life: whom you associate with, whom you hire, whom you promote, and whom you offer training opportunities to.

I've coached leaders at every level, from the C-suite to first-time managers, and I have facilitated over four thousand leadership workshops, executive coaching sessions, and training sessions. I've listened to participants' concerns and problems and I found that 99 percent of my clients' issues stem from a gap in EI and communication. This book focuses on communication as a process while also providing insights into EI. The goal is that you will use this book as a resource to assist you in increasing your self-awareness so that you can create clarity around who you are and why, how you show up, and why you think the way you do. I am sure all this talk about self-awareness and perspective sounds odd, considering the book is about courageous conversations. However, understanding who you are and why you think the way you do *is* the courageous part of the conversation. With a deep sense of self-awareness, you are more grounded in the purpose of your conversation. You are better able to regulate your emotions and navigate through emotional triggers. You are capable and remain focused on your values and goals of the conversation. This approach allows you to own your portion of the dialogue and focus on outcomes and solutions versus getting caught in an emotional spiral.

# Effective Communication Is Key

What is communication? Since it is something we do every day, it seems like an absurd question. But communication is a skill that we often take for granted. We seem to automatically identify those times when we have to slow down and engage in a real conversation. You know the times when you have to think through what you will say and how you will say it. That is when we are aware that it will require more effort to have *this* conversation. Communication is easy. Effective communication is the challenge. Effective communication is both a skill and an art. Effective communication is the process of exchanging ideas, thoughts, opinions, knowledge, and data so that the message is received and understood with clarity and purpose. When we communicate effectively, both the sender and receiver feel satisfied.[1]

Effective communication is a dynamic and complex art because of the unique perspectives we bring into the conversation. The challenges come into play when we interact with people who are different from us and have contrasting experiences, perspectives, and beliefs. Most often, everyone will have disparate opinions. Think of the earlier story about the gentleman who grew up in a strict religious family. Without knowing his background, you might think some of his perspectives, views, and opinions were absurd. Everyone comes to the conversation table with their backpacks full of everything they were taught and, unfortunately, only equipped with the things they have experienced or seen. These experiences that shape our perspective simultaneously make communication tricky.

During my research, I realized that there were tons of buzz phrases to describe communicating with someone with a different opinion than your own. Yet, there was little understanding of how to overcome those difficulties. Divergent opinions and courageous conversations topped those lists of hard-to-pindown descriptors. I quickly ascertained that there are no textbook definitions or frameworks with practical solutions for having effective, courageous conversations when divergent opinions exist that considered EI. I consulted everything from research articles to my doctoral program notes to the world wide web, all the way down to Twitter, but could not find a single definitive explanation or framework of how to have these courageous conversations through the lens of EI. Since necessity is the mother of invention, I decided it was time to redefine those terms and provide a framework for my practice. As a result, I compiled a myriad of research and simplified it into one palatable framework.

For our purposes, a divergence is any difference between two or more people's attitudes, opinions, or world views. Political party affiliations, immigration, climate change, religion, human rights, women's rights, gun control, how we raise our kids, who's responsible for what in a marriage, and who should clean the house is a small sampling of common divergent topics. Somewhere along the way and with certain topics, the term *divergent* has become synonymous with *divisive*. Today, more than ever, expressing your opinion can be so unpopular that it can lead to verbal altercations, ruined relationships, family divides, and even physical violence. As a result, we often choose avoidance as a strategy because of the anxiety we feel over addressing our differences, and the high risk we have associated. We then choose the "safe path" and decide that there can be no argument if there's no conversation in the first place. The challenging part of an avoidant approach is that we find no solutions. There are a lot of significant social issues that we all need to address. The point where we decide to engage and have a conversation or not is where the concept of courageous conversations comes into action.

The term *courageous conversation* is not new or groundbreaking. It became more popular after the death of George Floyd, when organizations wanted to create "safe spaces" for their employees to have courageous conversations about race and other social issues. Collectively, we identified that these issues were having a profound impact on employees' mental health and well-being. And these conversations don't just sit in organizational spaces. Over the past few years, I have seen these issues destroy relationships and tear families apart. So I thought it was time to identify a way for society to have a different dialogue.

## What Is a Courageous Conversation?

I define a courageous conversation as any conversation you don't want to have. Scott Buxton of the *Physiospot* website adds more depth to my thoughts and describes it this way:

> A courageous conversation is a discussion that is often difficult and uncomfortable. There are often emotions on both sides of the conversation and can be awkward, stressful, or challenging situations.[2]

I intrinsically knew that both definitions of courageous conversation were correct, but I felt something was missing . I remembered something I was told long ago: "Courage is only necessary where fear exists." In other words, you do not need courage when no fear exists. The missing piece was understanding the "fear factor" in a courageous conversation. Fear is an emotion that creates an instinctual pause or retreat response—flight, fight, or freeze. However, the goal is to go against your natural instincts and feel the fear. Not only feel it, but push through it with courage to have the tough conversations. As humans, it is always recommended to have reference points to help us understand our true capabilities. If I just tell you, "You got this," or "You can do this," that is not enough. Self-reflection and identifying moments where you have chosen courage over fear is important.

When the brain is triggered, and fear is the response, it tells the body to retreat. When we get uncomfortable with a conversation, we tend to avoid the conversation altogether. It's important to understand that this is the point of choice. We can choose fear and retreat from discomfort, or we can choose courage and engage in a thoughtful way. During my training sessions, I tell people to get *comfortable with being uncomfortable.* This is essential because we are learning to intentionally go against our instinct to choose safety. Choosing to stay in comfort, unfortunately, doesn't allow us much room to grow. Anything new will be uncomfortable. Intentionally moving into those spaces with courage is where we grow. When we feel discomfort, it is often because something is unfamiliar or uncertain to us.

I frequently give an example to help people understand how fear and courage work mentally and physiologically. (Please forgive me if this example triggers you in any way.) Imagine you are at a pool party with your child. As a kid, you had a traumatic experience while swimming in the ocean during a family vacation. Since then, you have not been in a body of water. While at the pool party, you are keeping a watchful eye on your child as they swim and play with their friends. However, while talking to another parent, you hear the distressed voice of your child. You quickly turn around and see your child struggling to keep their head above water. What do you do?

I've asked this question in training classes thousands of times. Every session, every audience member answers, "I would jump in." Of course you would! You would because the "why" moves you beyond your fear. This instinct tells us that we *can* move beyond our fear and do anything if we are moved strongly enough by the "why" that sits on the other side. We want to apply that same premise to courageous conversations. I implore you to push through your fear of having difficult conversations and make the conscious choice to engage because courageous conversations are necessary. When it comes to social issues, courageous conversations are vital for our society to identify solutions to big challenges. In our personal lives, courageous conversations are beneficial and necessary because they create more authentic and trusting relationships grounded in mutual understanding and clarity.

Since fear is the basis for avoiding difficult conversations, the question becomes, what are you afraid of? What makes you not want to have the conversation? In the previous example, a child's life was a powerful reason to move beyond fear. So now the question you must ask is: What is important about courageous conversations with people with divergent opinions and perspectives around important topics? The payoff for having a courageous conversation about divergent opinions is growth.

Last year I was working with a client, Jen. She was going through a difficult time in her marriage, and the stress from her home life was beginning to impact her job. She was used to a mindset of going along to get along, or "if I avoid it, it will go away." However, in this situation, she realized that avoiding the courageous conversations she needed to have with her partner was not helping. In fact, it was negatively impacting her mental health and her effectiveness at work. After several weeks of sessions, as tough as it was, she found her why and reason to push through the fear and talked to her partner. She told me, "What I am realizing is when I feel the fear and hesitation, that is a signal that I *need* to have the conversation. That my fear of rejection, abandonment, or being alone cannot stop me from having the necessary conversations and facing whatever the outcome may be." It was a powerful moment for Jen. Finding the *why* is like finding your North Star. It sparks your motivation and provides the boost of confidence necessary to have those difficult conversations.

Another aspect of fearing courageous conversation is past difficult conversation experiences. Ask yourself: *In the past, when I have had a difficult conversation with someone with a divergent opinion, what happened? Why? What was the outcome or impact on the relationship? How have I seen others engage in difficult conversations?* Asking yourself these three questions will help you understand the mental model you have created about courageous conversations and allow you to see where some of your fears and hesitations may stem from.

One day I was working with a client and walking her through the possibility of having a courageous conversation with her daughter. She looked at me and realized she had avoided many meaningful conversations because she feared how others would see her. She would rather be quiet than risk negatively impacting or losing the relationship. After some work and self-reflection, she realized how her past shaped her present. She used to be a talkative child. However, she grew up in a household where her parents constantly fought and yelled. She never saw constructive dialogue. Her parents divorced when she was ten. Over time, she lost her voice. As a result, she associated divergent opinions with conflict, and she deemed any divisive conversation as unsafe and avoided them at all costs.

As we see from these two examples, our past negative experiences can create fear and avoidance. They can also be used as learning opportunities. When it comes to courageous conversations around divergent opinions, my clients often describe the conversations as a conflict, argument, or debate. A courageous conversation should not be a debate or an argument. Instead, conversations with people who have divergent opinions and perspectives around important topics should end with expanded perspectives. The goal of a courageous conversation is never to try to change anyone's mind or force our beliefs and opinion on them. Instead, the goal of a courageous conversation should be about collective curiosity and the expansion of perspectives on both sides. The goal is to make space for different perspectives while being able to walk away and still hold your opinion.

## Divergent Opinions

Unlike divisiveness and its negative connotations, there's nothing wrong with divergent perspectives. There is never any progress unless someone first says, "I think it would be better if we stopped doing X and tried doing Y instead." Divergence should be about generating multiple creative solutions to problems or expanding everyone's point of view on topics. A fluid, nonlinear, more creative, mental state is achieved when we dig into divergent thinking and courageous conversations. It is this curiosity that is common among children. Divergence leads to imagination and fresh new perspectives that enable growth and positive change.

Part of the equation to having courageous conversations is increasing our EI. Remember, EI is learning how to effectively acknowledge, identify (in ourselves and others), and communicate the emotions we bring into a conversation. Those emotional components include biases, past traumas, and a boatload of other factors we'll discuss. We will learn techniques for self-awareness, self-regulation, and social skills to understand and connect with others. The result of learning these techniques is discovering how to respond based on your values, not in reaction to what your partner said or did.

As we review these concepts moving forward, it will be helpful to understand what your baseline is regarding divergent opinions and courageous conversations. I ask that you take a few minutes to take this self-awareness assessment. Rate yourself on a one-to-five-point scale for each of the statements below, one being low and five being high. The evaluation isn't a pop-psychology magazine quiz that will tell you what type of person you are. The goal is to make you aware of how to best utilize the contents of this book to help you initiate courageous conversations. If you score low, read this book with a mind toward development—a growth mindset. If your score is high, you will have an eye to refining your techniques and adding additional tools for approaching difficult conversations.

1. I am comfortable and confident engaging with people who are different from me.

2. I have intentionally reflected on my past experiences and understand what my perspectives are and how they were formed.

3. I am mindful of my blind spots and understand where I may have limited perspective, and continually self-evaluate to ensure I am open to learning new things.

4. I am comfortable engaging in conversations with others about diverse issues such as race, gender, sexual orientation, etc.

5. I am aware of my emotions/feelings around major social issues and why I feel the way I feel.

No matter where you fall in the self-assessment, our goal is not to make you comfortable with having courageous conversations. Since the definition of a courageous conversation is a talk that you don't want to have, you will always be a bit uncomfortable having these conversations. The goal is to help you get comfortable being uncomfortable. After reading this book, my hope is that you come away with techniques to elevate your competence and confidence when engaging in courageous conversations and practical tools to assist you in the process. I promise the reward of deeper understanding, increased perspective, and richer, more trusting relations will be worth the discomfort.

## The ACTER Model

While I know that sounds like a tall order, I developed a model to take the sting out of courageous conversations about divergent opinions. I call it the ACTER model, and I've been teaching it for years as part of my diversity and inclusion training classes. ACTER stands for:

**A**—Appreciating diversity of opinions

 **C**—Curiosity

 **T**—Triggers

 **E**—Emotional regulation

 **R**—Respectful listening

Please note, although the acronym is ACTER, there is no expectation of you being false or inauthentic in any way. On the contrary, the model allows you such a heightened sense of self-awareness that you build the necessary tools and skills that allow you to show up more authentic and more true to yourself in any conversation.

Each step of the model builds on the prior and will give you a mental framework to help you engage in courageous conversations. ACTER is not a method to manage your conversation partner's responses or help you "win" a debate. It is also not meant to be a step-by-step guide for every courageous conversation you have. After all, conversations don't typically fit into tidy, manageable packages. Instead, the ACTER model is designed to take the stress out of your side of the conversation to objectively hear your conversation partner's point of view. The model allows you to analyze yourself and manage your emotions. The more quickly you can clear away the emotional clutter surrounding conversations with divergent opinions, the easier it will be for you to develop the curious mindset necessary to conquer it. The world is clearer when you aren't defensive about what someone else is saying and you take the approach that you can learn something from everyone. In curiosity, we grow, learn, expand our perspective, and ultimately find our true selves.

The rest of this book will examine each of the elements in the ACTER model. Each step of ACTER is based on sound psychological tenets that form the basis of each point. These citations and principles come from professionals who have put in hundreds or thousands of hours studying, experimenting, and participating in the peer review process in their fields. I would be remiss if I did not apply their expertise in the development of the ACTER model. But this isn't solely a book based on theory, I also share real-world examples and conversation prompts to help you develop your skills in having any divergent-opinion conversation. As you continue to practice the ACTER model, you will find the framework is adaptable to your communication style. My goal is to teach you a methodology, not for you to be armed with canned responses. However, I've found that when learning any new skill, you have to master the basics before freestyling to meet your own needs.

Before you read any further, take a moment to review the self-assessment questions with a mind toward what you want to achieve with the ACTER model. Keeping those goals in mind when you read the next chapter, an overview of how to use this book, will assist you in personalizing the ACTER approach. Whatever your goals, I assure you that you'll achieve those objectives and more with an open and change-oriented mind.

# CHAPTER 1

---

# How to Use This Book

I encourage you to use this book as a guide. When learning any skill set, it is important to first develop the vocabulary and mindset along with those new capabilities. Let's say you want to learn how to play golf. You might familiarize yourself with golfing terms like *par, bunker,* or *backswing* to create a frame of reference for learning how to play the game. You also need to adjust your mindset to the scoring system in golf. Almost every other game you've played operates on a standard where the highest score wins. In golf, the game's objective is to take the fewest strokes to get your ball in the hole. That means in golf, the lowest score wins. You could look at a scorecard and pronounce an incorrect winner if you're not attuned to that mindset.

You've already started your journey to successfully conducting courageous conversations by learning some basic vocabulary in this book's introduction. Other terms will be presented in their proper context throughout the rest of the book and I've included a short glossary at the end in case you need a refresher on a term or concept. It also might be helpful to keep a notebook close at hand. Many of my clients find it useful to make note of terms or concepts they want to explore further.

Aside from defining key terms, it is paramount to explore how to assess and recognize that you may have to change your mindset and then apply the ACTER model to courageous conversations. I often see my clients believe that the ACTER model only applies to societal issues like racism, sexism, politics, and other similar topics. While the ACTER model perfectly suits those discussions, I've designed ACTER to address any courageous conversation. Remember that courageous conversations are *any* discussion you don't want to have. Setting boundaries, providing feedback to employees, and discussing a household budget with your partner are all examples of courageous conversations you have every day.

## Practicing Skills and Starting Out Easy

Since courageous conversations are all around us, we must adjust our mindsets to recognize these commonplace discussions as opportunities. If you start practicing the ACTER model in lower-stakes situations, you'll have a learning laboratory to practice your skills. It's much easier to start using the ACTER model when faced with the question of "Where should we have dinner?" than "Who are you voting for in the next election?" Remember that when you find yourself rolling your eyes, getting annoyed, emotionally triggered, or simply not wanting to have a conversation, that is the perfect chance to practice ACTER.

Building your confidence in lower-pressure conversations will allow you to adapt the ACTER model to your needs. I refer to ACTER as a model or framework because it is a guide. The reality is that there is no one-size-fits-all solution or technique for every situation. To further complicate matters, divergent opinions will differ from person to person or community to community. Different social groups face various problems due to varying experiences, socioeconomic differences, mores, and even geography. You must be agile enough in your approach to courageous conversations to recognize and navigate these differences. I've designed the ACTER model to be general enough to apply to any conversation you might have, while providing specific enough strategies to allow you to communicate effectively when divergent opinions are present.

Practicing your newfound ACTER skills is a hollow gesture unless we set goals for those skills. Most of us are familiar with goal-setting relating to our personal lives and careers. Your boss probably sets performance expectations for your job role that are measured in some fashion—the number of sales calls you make daily, client satisfaction ratings, and the like. These goals are easy to wrap your mind around because they are tied to specific external outcomes. The goals you will set with ACTER might be a bit more challenging to pin down because these goals are internal and relate to how you conduct yourself during a courageous conversation.

## Self Awareness

The first internal goal we touched on in the introduction is worth exploring further: how to manage yourself. In the Emotional Regulation chapter, we'll go into more detail on handling yourself, but it's important to plant some seeds early in the process. Before your next courageous conversation, you should examine how you acted during your last divergent-opinion conversation. Did you retreat? If you chose to engage, did you let your emotions get the best of you? Did you make statements you now regret? Were you more concerned with being right than understanding your conversation partner's point of view? There are invisible psychological forces that live beneath the surface of your psyche that cause these reactions. Unless you have the fortitude to examine how and why you react as you do during a courageous conversation, it will be challenging to have fruitful discussions with people you don't see eye-to-eye with.

It's not easy to search for why we react in conversations the way we do, and unpacking the root causes may bring up painful memories. Taking a complete inventory of your biases, traumas, and beliefs is beyond the scope of this book. Still, I would strongly suggest making that "first conversation with yourself" as honest as possible. One of my participants approached me after a seminar and said he was generally combative when having conversations that resulted in unfavorable feedback or criticism of his work. We spoke for a moment, and I found out that his mother was highly critical while he grew up. One story he relayed was that his mother instructed him to vacuum the den while she went to the store. The young man dutifully did as his mother instructed. When his mother returned, she relentlessly chastised her son for not following her instructions and made him vacuum the floor again. Her rationale was that the tracks from the vacuum cleaner were not going in the same direction on the carpet, so he didn't do the task correctly. This moment taught him that things must be done "perfectly."

The carpet vacuuming example borders on therapeutic but speaks to the level of introspection and self-awareness one needs to hold a courageous conversation successfully. This reflection on his childhood showed him where and why he is more likely to become triggered. The aim is not to solve the root problems but to be aware of them and understand how they affect your conversation habits. The young man in the vacuum-cleaning example has more profound issues to resolve about criticism. Still, he now knows he will likely respond poorly to any negative feedback. Armed with that knowledge, he can work to rein in emotional responses to criticism.

## Fixed and Growth Mindsets

When we recognize internal flaws and work to mitigate or overcome those impulses, we are knocking at the second goal of creating a successful courageous conversation—adopting a mindset that will make having courageous conversations easier. Mindset, in general, is easy to define. It's a group of traits that make up how we think about the world. A mindset is everything that goes into having that first conversation with yourself. Each of the ACTER model steps is also dependent on you having the correct mindset. You might think about adopting a mindset like all those times you were a child and *said* the right thing to your parents, but obviously didn't mean it.

"Apologize to your brother for putting toothpaste in his shoes."

With the appropriate eye roll, the child says to her brother, "I'm sooooo sorry that I squeezed a tube of toothpaste in your shoes after you hid my homework."

The child's apology was obviously not sincere because she did not have the proper mindset. The same principle holds true when you're having a courageous conversation. You can parrot every conversation prompt this book has to offer, but if you don't adopt the proper mindset, your conversation partner will be able to tell that you're being disingenuous. There are two overarching mindsets that work in the background of our mental processes—fixed and growth. This is notable from the research of Carol Dweck in her book *Mindsets* and is worth a read if you want to dive deep into the subject.

People with a fixed mindset believe that their talents and intelligence are fixed at birth, and nothing can be done about that. Holding a fixed mindset means believing that the mix of nature and nurture that created who you are can never be changed. You are who you are, and that's that. If you think of yourself in those terms, you have a fixed mindset. Having a fixed mindset isn't only about your self-image—it permeates your beliefs. To maintain your mental status quo, you must be right about everything. The concept isn't called *fixed* on a whim. Someone with a fixed mindset has built a mental tower of "correct" thoughts. If just one or two bricks of that tower are knocked out of place, the whole structure of one's identity can come crashing down. Often, this is rooted in perfectionism, fear of failure, or fear of rejection. This mindset creates boundaries for our personal growth and expanded understanding.[3] When one adopts a fixed mindset, they are never the best version of themselves.

Predictably, a growth mindset is the exact opposite of a fixed mindset. Someone with a growth mindset likes to challenge themselves because difficulties promote development. They see every day as an opportunity to learn, refine a skill, or seek out something new. A growth mindset is about transformation and understanding that anything significant in life can't be accomplished without dedication and hard work. Most importantly, a growth mindset says it's okay to be wrong or not know something because every misstep is an opportunity to improve yourself.

Please keep in mind that you are never always one mindset or the other. In my work, I've discovered that holding a growth versus a fixed mindset is situational. I notice that people are fixed in certain aspects of life while in a growth mindset in others. Many of my clients are very successful, top-of-their-class, and leaders of the pack. They have gracefully climbed the ladder of corporate America and conquered and survived many adversities and challenges along the way. In their professional lives, they see themselves as having a growth mindset. Their ability to continually build their skills, take risks, and take on new challenges is evidence of this. However, many of these same people have a fixed perspective about courageous conversations. The reason for this is often rooted in fear. Fear of the unknown. Fear of saying the wrong thing. Fear of their reputation and perception. Fear of being wrong or being challenged. Fear of offending the other person. Even fear of their own emotions. As we mentioned earlier, fear is a powerful emotion and fear will affect our mindset and our ability to have courageous conversations.

Perfectionism is a key driver of a fixed mindset. So, we will retreat from a courageous conversation and not say anything for fear of saying the wrong thing. Let's address the elephant in the room. As a result of "cancel culture," the fear of saying the wrong thing is more of a reality than ever. Cancel culture is *"a movement to remove celebrity status or esteem from a person, place, or thing based on offensive behavior or transgression."*[4]

What cancel culture has unintentionally transformed us into is a society where making mistakes is no longer acceptable. We live in an environment where it appears everyone is faster to be demeaning than to be curious. Cancel culture does not take into account a person's journey or growth. This is not to say that we should not hold people accountable as a society. However, the ramifications of swift cancel culture include a civilization of fear and the removal of constructive dialogue about important social topics. Cultures centered on fear do not allow room for any error. Unfortunately, when it comes to courageous conversations, you will make mistakes. It won't be perfect, and you must give yourself and your conversation partner space to be human.

Many of us grew up being scolded for discussing race, politics, sex, and other hot-button topics. As a result, these topics have been deemed taboo. Many of us do not have the experience or the competencies to discuss them effectively. As my grandmother used to tell me, "We have to give ourselves and one another some grace and mercy." Granny's advice is especially true when engaging in courageous conversations. When I start a conversation about a topic, I use statements that provide context for my engagement. I will use phrases like, "Forgive me, but I do not have much experience with or proximity to this. I am sure I will have a lot of questions." Another statement I often use is, "Forgive me if I say or ask anything offensive. Having these types of conversations is a bit difficult for me." I say this out loud to my conversation partner to create safety for myself and to make room for mistakes. This allows me to engage and remove the need to be perfect. Learning how to have or improve courageous conversations is like learning any new skill. If we are too fearful to try, we will never allow ourselves to make and grow from mistakes.

It's easy to see how a growth or a fixed mindset can affect a courageous conversation. If you have a conversation partner who has a fixed mindset, it will be tough to have them see the value of an opinion they do not hold. Conversely, if you have a fixed mindset, all the divergent-opinion conversations you have will be like fighting in a boxing ring. There is no way to have a productive, courageous conversation when every word is a punch. Progress happens only when we open ourselves up to the possibility that someone else's opinion and beliefs have merit.

Unfortunately, it's not always apparent whether you have a fixed or growth mindset. Someone could believe that they are open-minded and, yet, unknowingly shield themselves from new ideas. I like to think of this as the person who brings a ham and Swiss sandwich every day for lunch. Every so often, our ham and Swiss brown-bagger switches it up by putting spicy brown mustard on their sandwich. Because our brown-bagger slightly changes their routine, they believe they're the king or queen of spontaneity. That, of course, is not the case, and they're actually exhibiting signs of a fixed mindset.

There's a short quiz below to assess where you are on the spectrum of fixed and growth mindsets. Answer each of these questions as true or false:

1. I am comfortable making mistakes.

2. I have a tendency to shy away from tasks/activities that are challenging.

3. I am prone to avoiding tasks/activities that I feel I am not good at.

4. I believe most people who are successful are "lucky."

5. When I make a mistake, I am comfortable sharing my mistakes with others to create a space of openness.

6. When people give me feedback on something that I have done incorrectly, I tend to get defensive or shut down.

9

7.  I am comfortable engaging in conversation with others about topics that I am not experienced in and look at it as an opportunity to learn something new.

8.  If I fail at something once, I tend not to try it again.

9.  I constantly seek feedback from others and use it to create more self-awareness and growth.

10. I believe that I can learn to do anything that I want.

11. I believe that challenges in life help me grow.

12. I believe some people are just naturally good at things while others are not.

Now, score yourself using the following key:

**Question 1** — True, 1 point. False, 0 points.
**Question 2** — True, 0 points. False, 1 point.
**Question 3** — True, 0 points. False, 1 point.
**Question 4** — True, 0 points. False, 1 point.
**Question 5** — True, 1 point. False, 0 points.
**Question 6** — True, 0 points. False, 1 point.
**Question 7** — True, 1 point. False, 0 points.
**Question 8** — True, 0 points. False, 1 point.
**Question 9** — True, 1 point. False, 0 points.
**Question 10** — True, 1 point. False, 0 points.
**Question 11** — True, 1 point. False, 0 points.
**Question 12** — True, 0 points. False, 1 point.

Count your score and use the following key to assess if you have a growth or fixed mindset.

**0–3 points:**    Strong tendency toward a fixed mindset.
**4–7 points:**    Blend of both fixed and growth mindset.
**8–12 points:**  Strong tendency toward a growth mindset.

If your quiz results were on the fixed mindset side, there is a surprisingly simple solution to accessing a growth mindset. Simply acknowledge that you have a fixed mindset and then evaluate how it negatively affects you. Once you take that first step, it becomes easy. You'll see the relationships you've burned and the self-care you've neglected by choosing to be stubborn and inflexible in a dynamic world. Making that leap in self-awareness is another instance where you'll need courage. Admitting that you might not always be right is scary, but the benefit is an entire world opening up to you.

## Conversation Goals

In the introduction, I discussed why it takes courage to enter courageous conversations. Courage aptly describes an attribute we need to have in these conversations, but we must be careful of how we view being courageous. When you think of being courageous, some of the first mental images that come to mind might be standing up to someone or being brave in a life-threatening situation. These views of courage are correct but are counterproductive to our goals here. When we view any divergent-opinion conversation as conflict-based, we retreat into a fixed mindset where being correct or winning the fight is more important than understanding our conversation partner's point of view.

To keep your courageous conversation from straying into conflict, you first must have a conversation goal. Whether you know it or not, every courageous conversation you've ever had or will have falls into four different mindset subsets. This is different from growth versus fixed mindsets. These mindsets look at the approach we tend to take in a conversation based on our needs, values, insecurities, and fears. These mindsets are based on each conversation partner's level of competitiveness and defensiveness. Conversational mindsets aren't as quickly defined as fixed or growth mindsets. These mindsets can be dynamic based on the situation and conversation partner. However, given your personality, you are likely to tend to one of these conversation mindsets:

- **Win-Win Mindset**—This is the ultimate outcome of any courageous conversation and is an outcome that fosters collaboration between conversation partners. When we enter a win-win dialogue, it is based on the paradigm that there's plenty of room for everyone's opinion and one party's point of view doesn't threaten the other party. These discussions are respectful, and both conversation partners find merit in the other's statements. When we employ a win-win mindset, it becomes a philosophy of human interaction where everyone can succeed without tearing down someone else. If you've ever heard the adage "A rising tide raises all boats," you're familiar with a win-win mindset.

- **Lose-Lose Mindset**—Describes every horrendous cat-and-dog fight of a conversation you've ever been in. Conversations that are in a lose-lose headspace aren't conversations at all. They're rage-fueled arguments that can damage relationships. Both parties are thoroughly entrenched in their beliefs and can get vindictive. People with a lose-lose mindset are blind to everything except their desire for their conversation partner to be defeated, even if that means scorching the earth under their feet.

- **Win-Lose Mindset**—This mindset is drilled into our psyches at an early age through athletics and other games. We are taught that someone else has to lose for one person or team to win. An authoritarian approach says, "I get my way, but you don't get yours." A win-lose mindset often uses position, formal or informal power, and charisma to get its way. Trying to create a spirit of cooperation with a win-lose mindset is dysfunctional and can lead to resentment and damage to relationships.

- **Lose-Win Mindset**—It may be hard to understand how one party in a conversation willingly acquiesces their position to someone else. This happens when one of the parties is a people pleaser and wishes to gain popularity or acceptance. If someone adopts a lose-win mindset, they have little courage to express their feelings and are often taken advantage of by those employing a win-lose mindset.

When you enter a courageous conversation, you should strive for a win-win outcome. In most cases, courageous conversations are ideological in nature. You're probably not going to negotiate with a trade union or secure a parcel of land for your company (although the techniques in this text would be helpful in those areas). You're likely going to have a chat about religion, politics, race, or some other hot-button issue. During a single conversation, you aren't likely to sway someone's opinion or have yours changed. Those outcomes may happen in conversations eight or sixteen. But you're not even going to get to a second conversation if you're not respectful and showing an interest in your conversation partner's point of view.

The second reason you should keep conversation goals in mind when you enter a courageous conversation, is to identify where your conversation partner's head is during the conversation. You must recognize early in the conversation if your conversation partner's goal is win-lose so you can prepare yourself accordingly. We'll discuss specific strategies for this situation throughout the book, but for now, remember that you are only in control of yourself. Don't allow yourself to be baited into a knockdown, drag out screaming match if you recognize that your conversation partner wants to argue.

## Putting It All Together

Throughout the rest of the book, you'll be exposed to the individual elements of the ACTER model which will aid you in getting to that magical point of understanding and confidence. While learning the strategies that center around each of the critical points of the ACTER model, keep in mind the foundational lessons from this chapter. Sometimes you will think the content is too difficult for you to master and apply in a real-world setting. I assure you it's not, because that's the perspective of a fixed mindset. Your growth mindset tells you that even with this knowledge, every courageous conversation won't be perfect. However, you can choose to engage because you are now armed with a new vocabulary and tools that point you in the right direction. You'll know that when someone seems intent on grinding your gears in a conversation, they're looking for a win-lose endgame. You now have a name to categorize behaviors. When we name something, it becomes less scary than the unknown. Now it's time to use that growth mindset and learn some more.

This book aims to teach you how to build mature responses to uncomfortable situations that make you feel good about yourself while making it easier to have courageous conversations. This is a big objective, but it's worth stating because it has everything to do with you and little to do with your conversation partner. Every overarching concept we discussed in this chapter is an element that *you* control. How do *you* react in a conversation? Do *you* wake up every morning with a fixed or growth mindset? You set the conversation goals for a conversation. Your goal should always be to obtain a better understanding of your conversation partner's position. When we understand our conversation partner, we can empathize with their point of view. That's when all the magic starts to happen.

## Exercises and Examples

To help you obtain your magic moments, I've included a section at the end of each of the ACTER chapters called "Exercises and Examples." This section is designed to give you thought-provoking real-world examples of the principles you've read about, phrases that will help you navigate courageous conversations, and situations you can use to strategize how you can apply the ACTER model. Each section contains an interpersonal relationship and business/professional setting example. While these are not the only types of courageous conversations out there, I've chosen to avoid polarizing topics to help make this book as accessible as possible.

Of course, the situations in "Exercises and Examples" cannot cover everything. What these prompts and conversational simulations will do is create a new way of thinking about how to engage in a courageous conversation. The more you practice these skills, even by yourself, the better your chance is to use the ACTER model when it counts. I've seen clients come up with some ingenious ways to practice the ACTER model and utilize these exercises. Some of these methods include:

- Creating mock courageous conversations while commuting to work or during other travels.
- Journaling your responses and creating your own conversation prompts.
- Roleplaying a courageous conversation with a friend or family member.
- Seek out low-pressure courageous conversations. For example, strike up a conversation with someone who has a different method for reaching a goal, preparing a dish for a potluck, or listening to different music than yourself. Topics like these are seldom explosive and can give you an easy way to practice the ACTER model.
- Participate in online discussions with those who have different points of view than yours. When posting on a message board, you'll have the luxury of time to form responses that fit within the ACTER model. Yes, online discussions can become heated and are not for the faint of heart. Set your boundaries for how much is too much in online conversations, and stick to them. We'll discuss boundaries more in this book's "Triggers" chapter.

Now that you know the rules of the road for "Exercises and Examples," I've created a sample for this chapter. Use these sections at your discretion, but I promise you the more you practice, the smoother your courageous conversation will become. Now, let's get to work!

## Chapter 1—Exercises and Examples: How to Use This Book

Answer the following questions. I suggest writing your answers down and keeping them until you finish the book. Then come back and ask these questions of yourself again and see how your answers have changed.

How do you think the ACTER model will help you to have better courageous conversations?

_____

_____

_____

_____

What is your greatest fear about having a courageous conversation?

_____

_____

_____

_____

_____

Are there any topics that you find difficult to discuss with some-one else (politics, religion, race, sexual orientation, diversity in the workplace, setting boundaries, holding others accountable, etc.)? If there are, why do you have a problem with discussing these topics?

_____

_____

_____

_____

_____

Review each of the steps in the ACTER model from the introduc-tion. What step in the ACTER model do you believe will be the *least* useful to you, and why?

_____

_____

_____

_____

_____

Is there a specific courageous conversation you know you'll have in the future? If so, keep that in mind while learning about the ACTER model and make notes about which elements of each step will help you have that conversation.

_____

_____

_____

_____

_____

## CHAPTER 2

# A—Appreciating Diversity of Opinions

The A in the ACTER Model is Appreciating Diversity of Opinions. As we discussed in the introduction, everyone is different. We all have different histories, capabilities, and socio-economic starting points that make one person's story distinct from someone else's. This is something you should *know*, but do you *understand* how those distinctions can affect every aspect of someone's life? For our purposes, there is a massive difference between knowing and understanding a concept. I *know* that I can get on an airplane, and this machine will catapult me through the sky to my destination. Do I *understand* all the engineering and physics principles that allow powered flight? No.

As you begin your journey into the ACTER model, the first step is appreciating diversity of opinions. This means you must move from knowing we all have differences to understanding how everyone's thoughts differ. Those differences in views are what diversity, an often-maligned term, means. Diversity is the range of human differences and encompasses the understanding that everyone is unique and we can recognize and appreciate our differences. These differences can be along the dimensions of race, ethnicity, gender, sexual orientation, socioeconomic status, age, physical abilities, religious beliefs, political beliefs, or other ideologies. We also come from different backgrounds, have gone to different schools, and lived in different places. To move from *knowing* how we're all different to *understanding* those differences, we must first look at how everyone sees the world differently.

## The Challenge of Valuing Different Perceptions and Opinions

The driving element that keeps people from making meaningful connections is perception. Perception doesn't shape our reality. According to well-founded science, perception *is* our reality. This isn't just a philosophical statement, it's a truth of how your perception works. Before we get into the psychology of perception, I'd like to show you that perception and observation differ for everyone. On the next page, there is a collage. When you to turn the page, look at the image for fifteen seconds, put the book down, and then write down everything you remember seeing in as much detail as possible. Then, I would like you to conduct the same exercise with someone else. When you've both finished, compare your lists.

Based on my experience with this activity, I would say with 99 percent certainty that you and your friend's list were not the same. Even if you and your friend listed the same items, there's a high likelihood that you didn't describe them similarly. But why does this happen? You both looked at the same image. The question might initially sound silly and simplistic, but the answer gets to the heart of diversity of opinion and perspective. What you observe and how you describe the items are based on *your* perspective, your unique experiences, your upbringing, your education, your age, and a host of other factors that are unique to *you*.

The collage experiment not only highlights how our differences make us see the world differently; we can extract the value of diversity from this experiment too. Imagine you were asked to assemble a five-member team to perform the collage experiment. The task is the same—view the collage for fifteen seconds, and each team member writes down what they saw with as much detail as possible. Here's the catch. You are awarded a $10,000 prize for every item your team members precisely identify. How would you construct your team? Would you get people with the same background as you, or would you try to find people with a broad range of knowledge and experiences to fill your squad?

Suddenly, the diversity of your team matters, and everyone's observations and opinions matter. While you might normally discount the older team members' stories about back in the day, that same older person could identify the object appearing above the collage's center as a Rolodex. Someone who was born after 1990 might not even know what a Rolodex was. The artsy chick who goes to art crawls suddenly isn't so odd when she can identify da Vinci's *Mona Lisa* and Michelangelo's *David* statue. You could care less about cars, but you'll hug the car guy who makes you $10,000 richer for knowing the model and year of the yellow Ferrari.

The team collage experiment has real-world examples. In business settings, companies ranking in the top 25 percent of executive-board diversity were 35 percent more likely to outperform their industry averages financially. More diverse teams are also 87 percent more likely to make better long-term decisions.[5]

Diversity makes groups and individuals more creative, as well. A person's creativity is enhanced when they integrate different points of view. One of the ways integration happens is when we engage and interact with people from different backgrounds.[6] New research is coming out all the time that reinforces the benefits of diversity in everything from reducing friction between groups to faster problem-solving.[7]

If diversity is so beneficial, why is there such resistance to it? Part of the reason is that diversity isn't seen as a problem. People with a fixed mindset often believe that certain commonalities should result in the same opinions. Let's say I'm conducting a class in the United States and prompt the students, "Describe the ideological basis for America in less than ten words." The class might come to the consensus that the answer is life, liberty, and the pursuit of happiness. A fixed mindset would naturally assume life, liberty, and the pursuit of happiness meant the same to everyone else in the class. After all, we're all Americans and afforded the same opportunities—aren't we?

The belief that life, liberty, and the pursuit of happiness mean the same thing to everyone deals with perception. Not everyone sees the world the same, but some people do not recognize that. As shown in the collage exercise, each of us sees things through our own selective perception and filtered reality. In the late 1990s, psychologists Dr. Daniel Simons and Dr. Chris Chabris conducted an experiment that shows that what we pay attention to affects how we perceive the world. Participants in the study were shown a video of two teams of people passing a basketball between their teammates. The study's participants were tasked with counting how many times the ball was passed between team members. About halfway through the minute-long exercise, a person in a gorilla suit walks on screen. The gorilla takes a position in the middle of the action, dances around for a moment, and then walks off-screen. As the gorilla walked through their game, the team members passed the basketball around as if nothing extraordinary happened.[8]

After the video was completed, study participants were asked the following questions:

- Did you notice anything unusual while counting the passes?
- Did you notice anything else besides the players?
- Or did you notice anyone other than the players?
- Did you notice a gorilla?[9]

You would think that seeing a gorilla-suited person doing the hokey pokey would be the first thing the study's participants mentioned. It was not. Fifty-eight percent of the study's participants did not notice anything odd about the video.[10] More than half of the participants failed to see the gorilla, even though it was in plain sight. Psychologists call the "invisible gorilla" phenomenon selective attention. Our brains filter out large quantities of sensory information when laser-focused on a specific event, like counting the number of passes in a basketball game.

Selective attention isn't just limited to what we see. It also affects what happens to other senses. The invisible gorilla experiment was followed up a few years later by psychologist Dr. Polly Dalton of the Royal Holloway University of London. Dr. Dalton's study asked participants to listen to two separate conversations about the same topic. One of the conversations was between two men and the other between two women. In the middle of each conversation, a male voice said, "I am a gorilla," for nineteen seconds.

The gorilla did not go unnoticed in Dr. Dalton's experiment. Ninety percent of the study participants heard the gorilla man's voice during the male conversation. But, only 30 percent of the participants listened to the gorilla man's voice when listening to the women's conversation.[11] The research offered no explanation for why there was a marked difference between a male and female voice. Both gorilla experiments show that when humans focus on one thing, we can miss facts right in front of us. Think about the impact selective attention has on us in a courageous conversation.

Along with selective attention, several subconscious activities are important for us to be aware of when it comes to appreciating diversity of opinions. Our perspective is constantly at play, whether we acknowledge it or not. The key to mastering effective communication in any situation is our ability to have self-awareness. However, when emotions are high, it is not always easy to appreciate the differences of others, and there are some roadblocks that we must be aware of. Next, we will look at four valuable areas to analyze and be self-aware of to appreciate a diversity of opinion.

## 1. Separate Realities

As we just saw, selective attention causes considerable problems in the context of courageous conversations and how we interact with others. Let's further examine the implications of selective attention using the same hidden gorilla experiment. Suppose two people see the hidden gorilla video. Person A clearly noticed the gorilla walking through the footage. Person B missed the primate altogether because they were distracted by counting the number of times the ball was passed. Let's say we ask both viewers to tell us what they saw in the video. That conversation might start like this:

"I saw a group of people passing a basketball around. Then a gorilla stepped in the middle of the game, danced, and walked off."

"You're crazy. There were people playing ball, but there's no way a gorilla was in that video. I would have noticed that."

"I'm not crazy, but you must be blind. I saw it as plain as day. A person dressed in a gorilla suit walked right across the game."

"You're obviously trying to gaslight me. Seeing is believing. I didn't see a gorilla, so I'm not going to believe it was there."

Unfortunately, what usually happens at this point is the conversation disintegrates further because neither participant is willing to back down from their perspective of events. After all, each person holds on to a separate view of reality. For the moment, forget about anyone being right or wrong about the gorilla. Person A saw the gorilla, and that is real to them. Person B did not perceive the gorilla, which is equally valid. Yes, we could pause the video when the gorilla walked on screen and prove to Person B that there was a gorilla. The challenge is that proof has nothing to do with how Person B's perception worked (or didn't work) to recognize a gorilla. Person B's current reality is that there was no gorilla, and for the moment, we must accept that their perception can be valid without necessarily being correct.

We'll revisit correctness in a moment, but for now, let's discuss how Person A and B can both have their own realities. Without going down a philosophical rabbit hole, if we can agree that everyone's perception is different, no two individuals have the same reality of any given event. This difference in experience is called separate realities. Rabbi Shemuel ben Nachmani eloquently expressed the concept of separate realities by saying, "We do not see things as they are. We see things as we are."[12]

Practical examples of separate realities are all around us. Court proceedings are full of witnesses to a crime that recount different stories.[13] Referees see infractions during sporting events differently than we do on TV. Two people seeing the same movie will have different opinions about what they've seen. We're all in our bubble of reality shaped by our perception.

The problem stemming from separate realities isn't that they exist. The issue comes about when we do not acknowledge they exist. My grandmother used to always tell me, two people can have different perceptions about the same thing, and both be correct. As much as you may believe that everyone sees the world the way you do; or even want to believe the rest of the world would be better off if everyone thought as you did, that's not a healthy or realistic position. With this mindset, you can become trapped in believing something is wrong with either yourself or someone else for not having the same perception as you do. When you cannot conceive of anyone seeing things differently than you do, you can become defensive or even judgmental of the other person. When you do this, you cut off any chance at a meaningful dialogue. Consider Person A and B talking about the gorilla video. Each person was so convinced of their reality that they never considered the perception of the other or stopped to consider why they had seen different things.

Remember, we should avoid thinking our single reality or perspective is absolute truth. Based on our limited life experiences, we must acknowledge that there can be multiple truths regarding opinions and perspectives on any given topic. That is why a "yes ... and" mindset is so powerful. However, facts are facts. The fact is, there was a gorilla. In dialogue with others, we must leave space for an initial alternate reality and understand that it is plausible even when we see the same image or information. We may not see or understand the same thing. Consider starting your singular experience by saying, "based on my experience," "from what I could tell," or "speaking only from my opinion/perspective." These types of statements let your conversation partner know that you acknowledge that your perspective is not absolute and allow for different perspectives to be shared.

## 2. The Need to Be Right

Part of the reason Person A and B never considered why they had different points of view about the gorilla video was a primal need to be right. The need to be correct is a pesky part of our perception that is so ingrained in our psyches that it's nearly a universal law. Our entire society is built on a framework of being correct. From an early age, we're thrown into an education system based solely on a model of correctness. Being right gets us good grades, and high marks equate to a better future. In our careers, the more tasks we perform correctly, the greater our access to promotions and prosperity for our families. For those who live in the United States, the need to be right is compounded because our society is based on competition. No one watches the Super Bowl to see which side exhibits the most team spirit. We watch the big game to see which side comes out on top.

If you are prone to a fixed mindset, discussing matters of opinion can feel more like a personal attack than a friendly chat. A fixed mindset can feel like a personal attack because you're more likely to associate these matters of opinion with your identity. It's not difficult to see how the need to be correct bleeds over into issues of opinion like politics, religion, or grapes being part of chicken salad. Let's use grapes in chicken salad as an example. A friend brings chicken salad over for a cookout. Someone at the event expresses their opinion that grapes have no place in chicken salad. A fixed mindset person may take that comment as a personal challenge to who they are instead of looking at it simply as a difference of preference or opinion. The reaction from the fixed mindset person is to vehemently defend their position on grapes being in chicken salad. While the world will not crumble if someone makes chicken salad with or without grapes, the fixed mindset person's ego may crumble because of the challenge to their identity.

Discussing grapes in chicken salad sounds ridiculous, but substituting politics, religion, or sexual orientation descriptors into a conversation rapidly changes matters. For those with a fixed mindset, hot-button topics like these become conversational hills to die on, and arguments are likely to ensue—the need to be right then becomes a shield. The rationale is that "being right" will validate a fixed mindset belief, and that person will be safe in the status quo. Often, we are so confident that we see things the right way when, in reality, we are operating in a world based on our selective point of view. The hidden gorilla experiment gives us a concrete example of how this works.

If you wish to be successful in a courageous conversation, you must put away the notion of being right. I can assure you that your well-planned talking points will not be persuasive enough to change someone's mind about anything in a single conversation. The ACTER model is designed to help you have conversations that create relationships—not to win a gold medal for the debate team. If you're not interested in having conversations four, five, or six with someone with a differing opinion than yours, you're looking to pick a fight. Once we understand that being right does not equate to happiness, we can have better meetings, relationships, conversations, results, and lives.

# 3. Selective Perception

Another pitfall that is important to be mindful of is selective perception. I'm sure you've had many conversations where someone's only goal was to be right. This happens so frequently that our minds develop something akin to calluses. As soon as your brain perceives a threat, your perception kicks in some defensive mechanisms. These mental shields can be as reflexive as jumping at a scary part of a movie or putting your hands in front of your face before a car crash. Our mental reflexes use data and experiences from our life to make sense of what we're experiencing. When those experiences borderline conflict or recall other trauma, the brain often takes a shortcut to sidestep getting hurt. You may never know that your mind is trying to protect itself by throwing up these walls.

One of these shields is called selective perception, and it is closely related to the concept of selective attention we learned about with the unseen gorilla experiment. Selective attention in the gorilla experiment allows our mind to focus on a particular input and filter out extraneous information. Selective perception follows the same lines of stimulus gatekeeping by hearing what you want in a message while ignoring opposing viewpoints. If you've ever overlooked or forgotten information that doesn't align with what you want to be accurate, your mind is using selective perception.

There are two distinct types of selective perception you're likely familiar with—perceptual vigilance and perceptual defense. Perceptual vigilance is when you notice something that you find significant. Let's say you're thinking of buying a specific model and color of a car, and suddenly you start seeing more of those types of cars on the road. Those cars aren't magically popping up wherever you're driving. You're more likely to notice those cars because of your brand preference. Your mind is simply reinforcing what you already want. Perceptual defense is precisely the opposite of perceptual vigilance. Instead of confirming what your mind wants to see, perceptual defense makes you avoid unpleasant information. If it's been a while since you've been to the dentist, you might turn your head when seeing dental procedures on TV or on social media.

A classic experiment from the 1950s shows how selective perception works in the real world. Segments of a particularly violent Dartmouth versus Princeton football game were shown to students from both Ivy League universities. The Princeton students reported seeing almost twice as many penalties committed by the Dartmouth football team as the Dartmouth students.[14] We see what we want to see. Neither group of students wanted to view their team in a poor light, so their brains sidestepped the facts. On a courageous conversation level, selective perception kicks in when we're in the thick of it. When your conversation partner mentions concrete facts or figures that contradict your position, you are more likely to totally ignore what they've just said. It's like trying to remember that your significant other said they were going to book club next Thursday night—the nugget of knowledge keeps slipping into the "you never told me that" file.

The only way to combat any selective perception during a courageous conversation is through focus. No matter how hard it may be when you feel your mind slipping from your conversation partner's message, keep listening to what they have to say. Repeating every sentence your conversation partner says in your mind is one way to stay on track. Another method is to repeat a fact back to your conversation partner to ensure you understand their point. Whatever methods you use to keep your selective perception, or any of the other mental shields we've discussed in this chapter, will take practice.

# 4. Perspective Blind Spots

The last potential challenge I want to bring to your attention is perspective blind spots. If you've thought the material in this chapter was nice to know but in no way applies to you, you likely have a blind spot bias. The American Psychological Association defines blind spot bias as "the tendency of people to see themselves as less susceptible to nonconscious predispositions and cognitive influences than others."[15] That's a fancy way of saying your stuff doesn't stink. Believing that you're less biased than other people can be a significant bias on its own. When you think you're immune to any biases, how could you possibly see any biases you have?

Dana Brownlee, in a recent *Forbes Magazine* article, "Dear White People: When You Say You 'Don't See Color,' This Is What We Really Hear," addresses a classic blind spot by using handedness as an example. Brownlee writes:

> Right-handed people probably don't notice that spiral notebooks, three-ring binders, credit card swipers, school desks, scissors, tape measures, and

34

many other everyday items are designed for right-handed people. Why not? Because they simply don't have to. They get to move through the world without thinking about any of these everyday nuisances for left-handed people because right-handed people are the default.[16]

If not recognizing there could possibly be a problem outside your frame of reference isn't a blind spot; I'm not sure what is.

Perspective blind spots are insidiously destructive in relationships and courageous conversations because they quietly get in the way of building trust. The challenge with perspective blind spots is our lack of awareness that past experiences influence current decision-making. We make decisions and draw conclusions based on personal and past experiences. As a result, we do not recognize that we may be approaching a topic with deep complexities from our own narrow experiences associated with that topic. Perspective blind spots cause us to minimize and filter the topic through our bite-size experiences. As a result, when speaking with someone else with a different perspective, we may reduce the experiences that they have had, lack empathy, or even judge.

I remember a moment of self-reflection when I recognized a blind spot of my own. I was conversing with a friend about her desire to quit her job and start a new career. I was excited to hear about my friend's new adventure, but I could hear the hesitation in her voice. I responded from my perspective and said, "Just do it. What's the worst that can happen?"

My friend affirmed my statement, and then politely terminated the conversation. Later she told me she wished I could see things from her perspective. At the time, I was married, and she was single. She shared with me that the risk of quitting her job was so great that it scared her, and she hated that I could not understand. I spoke from my blind spot and could not be curious or show empathy. Over time, I self-reflected and identified that I tend to engage in career risk-taking. Ultimately, it has paid off, but I used to look at others and judge why they couldn't "try." After years of self-evaluation and reflection, I realized that my ability to take risks stems from my childhood. My grandmother raised me. She was sixty when I was born, and she raised me to survive in her absence. She taught me to "jump off the cliff" and bet on myself. A perspective outside of that was a blind spot for me. That was not everyone's experience, nor is that normal or comfortable for everyone like it is for me. But once I was aware of it, I began to walk through the world with a higher sense of awareness. I can no longer put my expectations on others. [17]

Blind spots are the carbon monoxide of courageous conversations. Odorless, colorless, and tasteless carbon monoxide can kill if there is too much in the air. The only way you know if there are dangerous levels of carbon monoxide is to have a detector. You'll need a detector for blind spots, too, if you want to recognize and overcome them. The best blind spot detector is listening while in a courageous conversation. When someone tells you that you're missing a point or not seeing a situation realistically, do not off-handedly dismiss those statements. Your conversation partner could have hit on one of your blind spots that you would never have known otherwise.

The best way to start seeing blind spots is far outside any courageous conversation. You should take opportunities to be curious and educate yourself about topics you know nothing about. Watch a documentary about a group or subject you're unfamiliar with. Pick up a book or magazine written from a different perspective than the one you hold. If you hear about a band charting the Top 40 and have never heard them, listen to one of their songs. Talk to someone that looks different than you at a coffee shop. In short, getting outside of your comfort zones will expose more blind spots than hoping you'll see them on your own.

## How to Appreciate Someone's Message

How do we navigate all the pitfalls our perception uses to keep us from appreciating someone else's opinion in courageous conversations? Revisiting what it means to have a growth mindset is a significant first step to any courageous conversation. There is no "winning" a courageous conversation in conventional debate terms. You succeed in a courageous conversation by learning something about your conversation partner and your conversation partner learning about you. (Revisit the win-win mindset in the previous chapter if you need a refresher on conversational success.) If you apply a growth mindset, you will not avoid conversations that expose you to a different opinion. Remember that where opinions are concerned, not everyone sees the world the same way you do. Give your conversation partner the courtesy of accepting that their perception and experiences are just as valid as yours. This doesn't mean everyone has to have the same reality, just that you take someone else's truth at face value.

Another strategy to appreciate someone else's opinion is to pause the conversation to define your terms. Not everyone uses words the same way, and that alone can cause confusion. If we aren't clear on the words and ideas being expressed in our conversations, how can we be clear on the solutions? It only takes a moment to ask, "What does that term mean to you?" Not only are you showing interest in your conversation partner's opinion, but you're also signaling that it's okay to ask you what your choice of vocabulary means. The clearer everyone is on the vocabulary, the smoother the conversation will be.

You can also pregame any courageous conversation by identifying your perception's vulnerabilities to the filters, blind spots, and selective perceptions we've learned about in this chapter. After reading the descriptions of these mental shields, you should be able to identify which apply to you, if you're honest with yourself. You must be intentional about opening your mind to fully engage in courageous conversations; therefore, you'll need to learn how to limit mental roadblocks during a conversation. When you find yourself slipping into one of these behaviors—stop. There's no shame in being in the middle of a conversation and asking your conversation partner to repeat a point if one of your filters has kicked in. You can also ask your conversation partner to pause for a moment so you can digest what they've said. Start out by asking, "Let me see if I understand this," and repeat your conversation partner's last statement in your words. If they agree with your assessment, move on. If you've missed the mark, simply asking, "Can you give me a moment to think about what you just said?" may help you regain focus. It also signals to your conversation partner that you're interested in what they have to say.

In any conversation, participants want to know they've been heard and their opinion is respected. We often believe that our conversation partner wants us to try to relate their experience with one of our own. Judiciously expressing common ground can show your conversation partner that you appreciate what they say. Often, equating experiences can show a blind spot or selective perception on our part that can fall flat. Consider this snippet of a conversation:

"Sorry, I'm not myself today. I found out this morning my grandmother passed away," said Abby.

"Oh my gosh! I'm so sorry. My grandparents are still alive, but I had a cat who died when I was a kid. I know you must be devastated," replied Ken.

As comical as this interaction might sound, you've probably been privy to or heard a similar transaction. When someone equates a disproportionate or *non sequitur* experience in a courageous conversation, it shows the opposite of appreciation. Ken expects Abby to feel some kinship between them because Ken has offered up the loss of his cat. No matter how integral Katy Purry was to Ken's upbringing, it's doubtful Abby will equate his loss equates to that of a blood relative. Ken would have done better by offering condolences and assistance in Abby's trying time.

We'll discuss how to manage conversational expectations more in the "Triggers" chapter. For now, be sensitive to another assumption that takes away from appreciating someone's opinion: agreement. We often believe that to have a good conversation, everyone must agree with the conclusion. That's not always the case. You can be noncommittal on someone else's stance and still show respect for their message. Your conversation partner may think they've had the best conversation of their lives because you listened and respected what they were saying.

The early parts of this chapter on appreciating the opinion of others focused on how to clear away your mental funk so you can fully hear your conversation partner's message. That's the difficult part of the A stage of the ACTER model. The more accessible part of the A stage is showing active appreciation. Try comparing a courageous conversation to someone doing something nice for you. How grateful would you be if someone stopped to help you change a flat tire on a cold rainy night? You would likely fall all over yourself thanking that person for their time and kindness. When someone shares their opinion during a courageous conversation, they share their experiences and feelings. Indeed, being privy to a deeply held belief is worth more than getting one's hands dirty by changing a tire and needs to be acknowledged.

We show appreciation for someone else's opinion by simply being part of the conversation. That involves actively listening to what someone is saying and positively participating in the conversation. The final phase of the ACTER model, respectful listening, will cover some of these strategies in more detail. For now, remember that your conversation partner won't have a clue that you appreciate what they're saying if you don't tell them. Even when your conversation partner is exhibiting signs of bias, you can still show appreciation by using some of these phrases to move the conversation along:

- "Yes, and ..."
- "While we may have different views, I can see there is passion on both sides and that is always appreciated."
- "I want to hear your perspective in order to better understand ideas that are different from mine."
- "I so appreciate you sharing your thoughts and opinions with me."
- "I appreciate that our different backgrounds and experiences have led us to form different perspectives around this important topic."

Using phrases like this shows your conversation partner that you're interested in what they have to say. There is no greater way to show appreciation in a conversation than investment and genuine interest. Even when you don't know what to say, being sincere goes a long way toward showing appreciation. How would you feel if, in the middle of a courageous conversation, someone earnestly said, "I don't know that I understand everything you're saying—but I want to. Help me to see things from your point of view." Our relationships with coworkers at work and loved ones at home are enhanced when we come more from "the way I see it" or "my point of view," as opposed to "this is the way it is." Expressing a level of vulnerability that shows your conversation partner your intentions of discovering more shows appreciation for their opinion and your desire to learn more. In the next chapter, you'll learn how to keep the conversational ball rolling by engaging with this curiosity.

## Chapter 2—Exercises and Examples: Appreciating a Diversity of Opinion

### Exercise: Training Yourself to Appreciate Diversity of Opinion

Every topic we cover in this text is a skill. Every skill requires both training and application to become useful. A master woodworker didn't pick up her tools on day one and magically create a chest of drawers. Someone had to show her how to master dozens of skills first, and then she had to apply those skills to create a piece of furniture. You weren't born with an innate sense of appreciating a diversity of opinion. We can talk about how you "should" feel about diverse opinions all day, but you're going to have to take action if you want to apply that skill.

An easy, actionable step towards appreciating a diversity of opinion is to put yourself in new situations. The more you get out of your comfort zone, the easier it will become for you to accept that someone else's opinions are as valid as your own. Here are some suggestions:

- Attend a lecture about a topic you're unfamiliar with or where you do not agree with the speaker's point of view. Sit through the entire discussion just listening, and stay through to the end of the question-and-answer session.
- Go to an art museum, institution, or gallery that features a style of art that's not your cup of tea. Listen to what the other patrons are saying about the art, or ask why someone likes that style of art.

- Listen to the top three songs from a genre of music you don't normally listen to. After you've listened to these chart toppers, look up a music critic's review of each song or album.
- Join an online discussion group for a topic that holds a different point of view than yours. Every day for a week, read the new posts and do not respond.
- Go out to dinner one night at a restaurant that serves a type of food you've never had or is someplace you'd never thought about eating at before. Ask your server what their most popular appetizer is and try it.

If all these suggestions sound like a horrible idea to you—great! These situations are supposed to give you a bit of trepidation. The more you expose yourself to new and uncomfortable situations, the easier it will be to appreciate your conversation partner's differing points of view.

### *Examples*

**How do we plan for retirement?**

Al and Jane got married a few years ago and they're both pushing thirty. Both are professionals whose companies contribute to a 401(k) plan. Each spouse has a wildly different philosophy on savings, which has caused more than a few arguments. Jane was of the opinion that the couple should forgo going on big trips and avoid frivolous spending for the next three years. The money they saved would go toward maxing out the contributions to their retirement accounts. Jane's logic was that the compounding earnings in thirty-five years would more than make up for a few lean years now. Al's take on retirement was that they should make moderate contributions now, since they were both early in their careers. The future held promotions, raises, and bonuses that could be dumped into the nest egg for their twilight years. Al wanted to take advantage of their youth and make the most of life while they could.

The uncertainty of her husband's plan made Jane nervous. What if one of them got laid off? What if both of their careers didn't take off like Al thought they would? There were too many variables for Jane to consider and she usually shut Al down early in retirement planning conversations. She'd even drawn up financial projections for Al to show that her plan was sound. Still Al wouldn't budge. Jane's tactics were getting them no closer to a resolution, so she decided to adopt a growth mindset when discussing Al's vision for retirement. Jane set aside a quiet afternoon and promised that she'd be more open-minded to his plans. Let's listen in.

"We're getting nowhere on this retirement plan. We have different views, and I can see we're both passionate about our plans. I want you to know that I appreciate that passion and want to hear you out."

Surprisingly to Jane, Al had a well-thought-out projection for their future earnings. At the end of his spiel, Al threw in, "My parents always had a side hustle. They dumped all that money into their retirement. That's my safety net if our careers don't go like I planned. There's always something I can do to make sure we retire well. But I don't want to live like they did if we don't have to. Mom and Dad were always worn out looking for the payoff when they might be too old to enjoy it."

Jane thought about this for a moment. She didn't know that about Al's parents or that he had a plan B. Before interjecting anything about how their plans differed, Jane said, "I appreciate that our different backgrounds and experiences have led us to form different perspectives about retirement. I am looking at this from a position of security early on because of some things I saw growing up."

Jane went on to tell Al about how her childhood and parents' decisions formed her opinions about retirement. After they finished their discussion of why they felt the way they did, Jane said, "I appreciate you sharing your thoughts and opinions with me. Could we figure out a compromise that gives us both security and flexibility?"

Part of having any courageous conversation is being honest with your conversation partner. In this example, once both Al and Jane listened to why they had a diversity of opinion they had a starting point to make a plan. Sometimes all it takes is a little understanding to move past a roadblock.

## Boss, I've Got a Great Idea

Christy is a junior environmental, social, and governance (ESG) officer for a large mining operation. One of her chief job duties is pulling together all the mine's emissions testing results for government audits. Not only were the emissions results a regulatory requirement, but the company also received a tax credit for hitting certain emissions goals. To date, the mine's emissions only qualified the mine for the lowest level of tax savings. The operation was close to making the next bracket of tax savings but couldn't quite get there—until they implemented Christy's great idea. In an industry magazine, Christy saw an article on electric vehicles being used in mining operations. Doing this could surely decrease the mine's emissions, and the tax credit would more than pay for the new equipment.

Tom, Christy's boss, was inundated with ideas. Everyone from security guards to miners thought the ESG department was the company's suggestion box. Quite frankly, Tom was sick of hearing new ideas. He almost ran out of the cafeteria when a well-meaning payroll clerk suggested the mine could have a mascot like sports teams do. They could post Mitch the Miner on social media doing all sorts of funny things to increase the company's social currency. Tom wasn't amused and felt even less so when Christy asked him if he had a moment for a suggestion. Tom held his breath for a moment and remembered that one out of a hundred ideas were gold. Tom just hoped Mitch the Miner was the ninety-ninth idea of the day.

Christy started in with background of the emission tax credit and what the company's current savings were. Tom replied, "Yes, and ..."

With that opening, Christy threw out cost figures for electric vehicles, the emission tax credits, and an electric vehicle tax credit she'd just found out about. All of that together would increase the company's profits. When Christy paused to take a breath, Tom asked, "What else? You've got governance and environmental covered, but how do we sell this, given our mandate to improve the social appearance of the company?"

"Has Wendy in accounting told you about Mitch the Miner? We could have him drive the electric trucks around the mine," Christy said, tongue in cheek, before launching into a social media campaign plan for the new equipment being used on site.

Tom groaned at the reappearance of Mitch the Miner, but thought Christy's plan was solid and added, "I appreciate you sharing your thoughts and opinions with me. I'll look at the numbers and let's revisit this next week with the chief financial officer."

Appreciating a diversity of opinion isn't always easy. There are some days we're on information overload and the thought of hearing one more idea or opinion is like fingers on a chalkboard. Don't give in to being impolite simply because you've had enough for one day. Take a moment to hear someone out. If you truly don't have the bandwidth right then, make sure your conversation partner knows you want to hear them and schedule a time that you can appreciate what they have to say.

**CHAPTER 3**

# C—Curiosity

Before we delve into the next step of the ACTER model, let's take a quick step back to examine the motivation of any courageous conversation. We've defined a courageous conversation as any discussion you don't want to have. Usually, the participants have different points of view on the conversation topic. Politics, race, religion, sexual orientation, or one of the zillion other hot-button topics could be involved in a courageous conversation. While the points of view differ for each of the conversation's participants, one common ground is that the topic is vital to both participants.

If you're not interested in hearing why the topic is important to your conversation partner or what their solution to a specific problem is, why are you having the conversation? You're probably spoiling for a fight and need to disengage from the conversation. If you're genuinely interested in having your point of view heard and understood, you'll have to be ready to do the same for your conversation partner. You'd expect that your conversation partner would ask questions about points they didn't understand. You might want your conversation partner to ask why you feel so passionately about the topic or what led you to your point of view. If you expect that from your conversation partner, you should exhibit those elements of curiosity yourself.

Being curious is the next part of the ACTER model. Being curious in this model means entering conversations and relationships assuming you have something to learn—it's a mindset. If the goal is to have a productive dialogue with another person, we must suspend our judgment and approach the conversation with a curious mindset. You're not trying to push an agenda or change someone's mind on a topic. Every courageous conversation is a fact-finding mission. Curiosity, when speaking with someone you don't necessarily agree with, is a skill that must be actively honed and used. Our instinct is to shut down and stop a conversation when we start hearing things we disagree with. It's like walking toward a garbage can on a blazing summer day. You'll avoid the hot garbage smell even if it means walking half a block out of your way. You can't hold a successful courageous conversation without being curious about what's stinking in the trash can.

## Expansive Thinking

Curiosity is simultaneously the most critical step of the ACTER model and the most misunderstood. The stock definition of curiosity is wanting to learn, understand new things, and know how those things work.[18] That's a fine definition, but the assumption is often made that curiosity is an external exercise. If you flip a light switch and wonder how electricity is generated, that's a form of being curious about the world around you. You could even apply that definition to your conversation partner. If you enter a conversation believing you have something to learn, there's a natural level of curiosity that goes along with that growth mindset.

The goal of curiosity is to create expansive thinking. It is just as it sounds—the expansion of our understanding, a broadening of our perspective, and stretching beyond our horizons. Expansive thinking allows you to hold multiple realities simultaneously and moves you beyond your immediate personal context to enable you to look at things from various perspectives. Expansive thinking is an exploration process grounded in curiosity for the sole purpose of understanding the collective perspective and experiences of others. It is key to creativity, problem-solving, and creating flexibility in our mental model to find new discoveries.

Have you ever tried putting on a piece of clothing you haven't worn in a while, only to find out it's a little snugger than you remember? Is your first thought *I've put on a few pounds*? Or do you think, *Oh, that must have shrunk in the dryer*? Both explanations for the tight piece of clothing are equally plausible, but you are not being curious if you don't explore both options. You've closed yourself off to finding the real reason behind why those jeans don't fit. Maybe you put on a few pounds, *and* perhaps it shrank. The fact of the matter is both can be true simultaneously. This is what we call "yes and" thinking. It tells us that more than one reality and possibility can exist at the same time.

Curiosity grounded in expansive thinking is so valuable in a courageous conversation because it allows us to approach a topic with an understanding that there can be multiple realities and possibilities. Expansive thinking will enable you to move out of the singular reality of either-or, black and white, or static thinking, into complex, critical thinking.

The debate around global warming and climate change is a wonderful example of how expansive thinking can be applied to a specific topic. Some argue that carbon emissions and fossil fuels are causing global warming and destroying the planet. Others say nothing is wrong with climate change and it's a natural and regular cycle. This creates an either-or scenario. In an either-or scenario, we get stuck in a hard-to-identify solution. Either we do everything, or we do nothing. What if we used expansive thinking and asked the question, what if both are true? What if climate change and global warming are natural and normal, *and* we can look at our actions as humans and how to lessen our impact? History and data tell us the planet goes through cycles of climate change despite human interference. We can also identify how human behavior may add to and impact the normal process. Both can be true. The challenge exists when we refuse to expand our perspective through curiosity to have a thoughtful dialogue.

Our perspective reshapes and creates an expanded mental model when we engage in expansive thinking. Shaping our perspective through expansive thinking happens through active curiosity, exposure, and proximity. Have you ever wondered why politicians tour the country during election season, meet with families and citizens, and then eloquently share their "while at a dinner table in Boise" stories? These politicians are demonstrating expansive thinking by spending time with people from different backgrounds on their home turf. Remember, as humans, we only have limited experiences from which to draw our mental models of the world. However, when we hear the different lived experiences of others, we can gain a broader understanding and perspective of life. This holds true in every aspect of our life.

## Curiosity as a Mindset

Curiosity as a mindset isn't always easy. Even when instructing others on how to be curious, I find it difficult to be curious about myself and others. To remind myself how important curiosity is, I have a bright pink sticky note on my computer monitor that says, "BE CURIOUS!" Being curious and asking questions helps me minimize judgmental thinking and responses. I find that when I am curious, the amount of "per my last email" or "as you are no doubt aware" statements are reduced dramatically.

Since you can't always carry around a neon pink sticky note reminding yourself to be curious, I'd suggest making a slight revision to our definition of curiosity to encompass both external curiosity and internal self-awareness. Let's define curiosity as entering conversations and relationships assuming that you have something to learn by collecting data about yourself and others. Our new definition gives a firm basis for discovery while also reminding you to turn your eye inward.

With our new definition of curiosity, you're now ready to employ curiosity in your courageous conversations. As you do so, keep in mind that not everyone will have the same definition or concept of curiosity as you do. After reading this chapter, see if the above definition of curiosity matches with how you now perceive curiosity. When you're in a courageous conversation, you should consider what curiosity means to your conversation partner. They might not understand how to be curious in a conversation, and that's okay. Simply recognizing that fact will keep you from getting defensive if your conversation partner doesn't show the same level of curiosity in you as you've shown in them.

## Curiosity with Others

As we mentioned earlier, the biggest challenge with a courageous conversation is that each of us walks through the world with different lived experiences and, therefore, sees the world very differently. This means we can have very different perspectives and opinions about the same topic. Being curious about your conversation partner is the key to gaining an understanding of how they formulated their thoughts around the topic and better understanding their perspective. Curiosity with others is not used as a defense mechanism to shoot holes in their theories. Instead, curiosity with others is an active and intentional mindset that allows us to pause our brain and suspend judgment in order to gain insight into who they are and why they think the way that they do. When we do this, we are able to gain more insight and learn new things. Curiosity about others first starts with a willingness to listen intently in order to understand.

Curiosity should not just sit in isolation and be activated during a courageous conversation. Instead, curiosity should be seen as a mindset, a way of being—something that we implement in every aspect of our life for continuous learning and growth. To develop our curiosity skills, we must learn a few lessons from childhood, when our curiosity was at its peak. A few weeks ago, I boarded an airplane and sat next to a mother and her daughter. The adorable little girl couldn't have been a day over three. As we waited for the plane to taxi, it became obvious that this was her first time flying.

"How does the airplane stay in the air?" was the precocious girl's first question.

The mother tried to simplify the physics of flight for her daughter, but her answer didn't meet her daughter's expectations. Then came the inevitable question, "But why?"

I've always heard of the infinite questioning called "the why game." Anyone who has spent more than fifteen minutes with a preschooler knows how this game goes. No answer an adult gives completely covers what the child wants to know, so the child's only recourse is to continue asking, "But why?" Children play the "why game" because they're attempting to figure out the world around them. For the most part, children also accept the explanations adults give them. However, there are situations where a child will touch a stove even after they've been told it's hot, but I view that as another expression of curiosity. The child is curious about the meaning of what "hot" is and what will happen when they touch the hot thing—not because the child did not trust what the adult said.

If you wish to be successful at having courageous conversations, you must remember what it's like to be a child. The curiosity of a child is their primary mindset and driving motivation. Most of a child's activity is somehow rooted in trying to answer the hows and whys of their world. When you enter a courageous conversation, if you're not asking questions or listening most of the time, you're not doing it right. I promise that if you exhibit the proper level of curiosity, you'll both have ample time to have your say and better understand your conversation partner's position.

However, if you're only curious about your conversation partner, you're missing half of the equation. The same curiosity you extend to your conversation partner should be equally turned inward. That means you must be curious about yourself. That may sound silly at the outset. How can you be curious about yourself when you're the world's leading expert on you? It turns out that we are often not as aware of our motives and behaviors as we think we are.

## Curiosity with Self

In the introduction, I shared the intersection between emotional intelligence (EI) and courageous conversations. The first and most important aspect of EI is self-awareness. Self-awareness is a deep understanding of self. Curiosity is the vehicle of our self-awareness. Curiosity with self includes understanding your needs and emotions, what triggers you and why, your life experiences, and how your past experiences connect with the current conversation. Regarding courageous conversations, the goal of curiosity with ourselves is to understand better how we feel about and perceive a subject/topic. There are two aspects to explore—how we feel and how we perceive.

When we look at courageous conversations through the lens of EI, we understand that our emotions are the power drivers of our behaviors. Sometimes we aren't aware that we will have an emotional reaction to a topic until we get in the middle of a conversation. Then, these emotions will often surface and unintentionally derail an important discussion. Let me connect the dots. In my diversity and inclusion workshops, I show participants six images. These images represent social issues that we have all seen in recent years. The images are strong and can be emotionally triggering. The social issues collage includes pictures of:

- Social injustice
- War
- Gun Control / Gun Violence
- Affirmative Action
- Immigration
- Oppression of marginalized groups
- Women's reproductive rights

I ask them to look at the collage of images in silence for thirty seconds. As they look at each picture, I ask them to think about how the images make them feel. After thirty seconds, I remove the images and ask each to share one word to describe how the images make them feel. The lists are always insightful. Words such as *exhausted, frustrated, angry, sad, confused,* and *numb* always appear. Think about these emotional words—exhausted, frustrated, angry, and sad. These are powerful emotions. However, we rarely consider these emotions. Let's discuss why this is important to take into consideration. You want to engage with someone around immigration in the United States. Yet, you enter into the conversation unaware that you have strong emotions of anger or frustration attached to the topic. Without knowing what you feel about the topic and why, you are walking into an emotional minefield. It is essential to be curious about yourself to identify what emotions you have around a topic or issue before engaging in a courageous conversation. Don't stop with identifying the emotion. Dig a bit deeper and ask yourself why you feel that way.

During the height of the pandemic and social unrest, I had a colleague ask me about Black Lives Matter. As a person of color in the profession that I am in, I understood why they reached out to me. However, I found myself emotionally exhausted and drained. With this awareness, I shared with my colleague what I felt about the subject and why. Our conversation was more focused on the human experience than the divisiveness that sat inside the topic. Had I not been aware of my potential emotional responses, I could have allowed my anger and sadness over the senseless violence to enter the conversation. Being aware and owning the emotion we feel around a topic allows us to understand why we may be less engaging, more passionate, or more sensitive.

I see this in many parents regarding discussions around gun control. There is an emotional connection to the topic. Often the words they use are *frustrated* and *scared*. Imagine the passion a parent might display as they describe how they can't envision their child experiencing gun violence in a place they once considered safe. Yet another person might feel attacked and defensive because they feel their gun rights are being threatened in this debate. Both sets of feelings are valid and should be taken into consideration before you enter into a courageous conversation. The next time you watch or read the news, pay attention to your emotions. Instead of dismissing the reason you shook your head, or changed the channel, ask yourself, what am I feeling and why? This level of proactive self-awareness around the emotions we have tied to a topic is valuable in a courageous conversation, as it can support you in communicating your thoughts and perspectives clearly to your conversation partner and allow for more emotional regulation. We will dive into emotional regulation later in the framework.

## Integrating Curiosity as a Mindset

Why is curiosity so powerful? It's because curiosity impacts all levels of social interactions. Curious people are often viewed as more exciting and engaging by others. The curious are more likely to reach out to various people and are viewed as more intellectual. Also, when someone is curious about what you're doing or what you're about, it makes you feel noticed and significant. Social interactions borne of curiosity create bonds of intimacy that inevitably improve our relationships.[19]

Curiosity, like any mindset, must be actively practiced. If you don't make a point to intentionally integrate curiosity into your conversations, you'll never see it's full benefits. After one of my training sessions, a young lady approached me and asked for some off-brand help. She was fresh out of college and had snagged an outside sales position with her company. The first couple of months of making outside sales contacts wasn't going as well as she had hoped, and she wanted to know if I could critique her sales pitch. I love to help anyone starting out, and I agreed to listen.

This woman got into her pitch, and she was on fire. You would have thought she owned the company from how she spoke about the products she was repping. Prices, technical specs, and delivery times were given to me like she'd delivered this pitch a thousand times. Nothing I could find in her delivery was amiss—except for one thing. She was never curious about what problems the client was experiencing. A good salesperson knows everything about their product line. A great salesperson is curious about the business's challenges and how her products can be a solution. That's how salespeople create lasting relationships with clients—through curiosity.

I advised the young lady to put equal weight on asking questions to her clients as she did to memorizing the technical specifications. All it should take was four or five intelligently formed questions about her client's business. These questions didn't need to delve into proprietary information or processes. All she had to do was show an interest in how those businesses ran and practice those questions at crucial points during her sales pitch.

## Curiosity Is Also an Emotion

Curiosity is a complex emotion because more than one state is ascribed to "being curious." You pretty much know what you're in for when you identify your emotional state as happy or sad. When you're curious, you can feel frustrated, like in the TV show example. Or you can feel happy anticipation toward learning something you don't know yet.

The information gap model is a prominent psychological theory that fits our uses of curiosity in the ACTER system. This model suggests that you become curious about something when you notice a gap in your knowledge base. That gap between knowing and not knowing motivates you to bridge the divide by seeking new information. The information gap theory is much like hunger in how it affects you emotionally. Sometimes hunger causes you to get hangry, and other times you think *I want a good steak*. That's the difference between curiosity being a frustrating and enjoyable experience.[20]

The emotional components of curiosity play into a courageous conversation because they can change the entire mood of the conversation. Let's say that your conversation partner is asking you questions to ascertain your past experiences or how you came to your point of view. If you're being evasive, or simply not being as forthright as you could be, your conversation partner might become frustrated because they're curious. The same could hold true for you if your conversation partner does not satisfy your information gap.

If you know why you're having an emotional response to curiosity, you can take a simple step to ensure your feelings don't impact the conversation: set boundaries. If your conversation partner's curiosity is getting too personal, let them know. Make a statement: "I'm sorry, I want to have this conversation but that's something I'd rather not get into right now. Can we talk about something else related to our topic?" Conversely, if you sense you're being too curious about your conversation partner's tastes, ask if it's okay: "I'm sorry. Am I getting too personal? I'd like to understand where you're coming from. Are there better questions I should be asking?"

Setting boundaries is never an easy undertaking and takes the same courage you had to muster up to have the difficult conversation in the first place. The secret to setting conversational boundaries is to permit yourself to say what's enough. Having a courageous conversation doesn't mean you have to tell all you know. You and your conversation partner must ascertain what you are comfortable sharing. If you have rigid boundaries about specific topics, you can always state those at the beginning of the conversation. Don't forget to be curious! If you have boundaries, your conversation partner probably does too. Asking what their boundaries are will help you build trust and help you avoid conversational minefields.

## Curiosity Is the Opposite of Judgment

If our goal in a courageous conversation is to create understanding through curiosity, you need to know what will absolutely derail your efforts. We can identify several off-putting behaviors during a courageous conversation—apathy, disingenuousness, and dismissiveness, to name a few. You could name objectionable behaviors until the next sunrise, but you wouldn't get to the root of the problem. Every time you or your conversation partner exhibits poor conversational etiquette, it's because one of you has decided to do so.

That decision to be less than your best self in a conversation is a choice that we own. One of the most damning responses in a courageous conversation is being judgmental. When you are critical of someone's lifestyle, opinion, history, or any other aspect of your conversation partner's existence, you've made a judgment. Once you judge your conversation partner, you've shut down any chance at curiosity. Remember our definition of curiosity: entering conversations and relationships only assuming that you have something to learn by collecting data about yourself and your conversation partner. The moment you make a judgment, you believe you know everything there is to know about a situation or person. Being judgmental can also cause your conversation partner to become defensive or shut down. Judgments derail the actual point of the conversation and it becomes more about your conversation partner defending themselves than sharing their experiences and feelings. Think of making a judgment like flipping an ancient rusty light switch. Once the light is turned off, it's hard to flip the curiosity switch back on.

The difficulty in turning the curiosity switch on again isn't that you cannot recover from a momentary lapse in a conversation. The issue is that if you fall into a pattern of being judgmental, you're taking steps toward adopting a closed mindset. Think of having an open mindset as approaching an open doorway. Every time you make an unsubstantiated judgment, you move the door closer to being closed. Eventually, the doorway of an open mindset will be completely closed, affecting how you move through the rest of your life.

## Pitfalls of Being Judgmental

The detrimental effects of being judgmental don't end with stifling curiosity during a courageous conversation. Rushing to judgment can have far-reaching personal consequences, from impacting our interpersonal relations and keeping us from being able to understand one another to limiting our creativity and innovation. Consider the quotes below, which show how wrongheaded being judgmental can be.

- "Remote shopping, while entirely feasible, will certainly flop. It has no chance of success." (*Time Magazine, 1966.*)[21]
- "There's no chance that the iPhone is going to get any significant market share. No chance. It's a $500 subsidized item." (Steve Ballmer, CEO of Microsoft, 2007.)[22]
- "Mobile phones will absolutely never replace the wired telephone." (Marty Cooper, inventor of the mobile phone, 1981)[23]
- "There is no reason an individual would ever want a computer in their home." (Ken Olsen, founder of Digital Equipment Corporation, 1977.)[24]
- "Television will never hold onto an audience. People will very quickly get bored of staring at a plywood box every night." (Darryl Zanuck, cofounder of 20th Century Fox, 1946.)[25]

Legends within their fields made each of these statements. How could these visionaries possibly miss the ball so spectacularly that we're now focusing on their mistakes rather than their accomplishments? These men allowed their personal prejudices, biases, and perhaps even fears to form the basis of their judgment on technological markets. If you think you're more immune than the CEO of Microsoft or the inventor of the cell phone to making poor judgments, you're wrong. We are all capable of letting the same factors that caused these poor predictions to taint our own worldviews.

Making judgments can be worse than getting a little ribbing about making a wrong prediction. Being judgmental affects how we make sense of the world and make decisions. If you are in the habit of making blanket statements or speaking in absolute terms, you'll miss out on creative solutions to problems. You also run the risk of inadvertently hurting someone's feelings or destroying a relationship. Judgment is the opposite of curiosity. Finally, the more you judge others, the more you will be critical of yourself. Imagine the last time you were overly judgmental and heaped that type of judgment on yourself. Eventually, that level of self-criticism will lead to internal conflicts and undue stress. Give yourself and everyone else a break and keep an open mind.

## Judgmental Mindsets and Behaviors

No one wants to think they're being judgmental, but sometimes everyone irrationally disapproves of someone or something. That vicious inner monologue says things like: *What was she thinking wearing that? He should not have gotten that haircut. They're just together because he's rich.* The devil sitting on our shoulders feeds our imaginations' negative commentary nearly reflexively. Humans have strong feelings about what we perceive as right or wrong. We know immediately if we like or despise something for no reason other than "because." The truth of the matter is we all judge. It's a part of our human condition. Judgment is a natural survival instinct or defense mechanism. According to High Country Behavioral Health clinical director Tiffany Hogue, in our primitive phase, we used judgment to evaluate threats or dangers. She says this about judgment in the twenty-first century:

Sometimes they [judgments] can keep us safe, and some say that they exist to keep us safe. In history, if a tribe member is going against tribe beliefs or putting the tribe in danger, judgements were made and that person was exiled—which, in turn, kept everyone safe and alive. Also, in today's world, there is a place for judgement (and judges) on right versus wrong. The problem exists when these judgements are not factual and/or not necessary.[26]

This is why it's practically impossible to stop making *any* judgments, and I'm not suggesting that you try. There are situations when making a quick judgment call without complete information, is necessary. I'm suggesting that in the context of courageous conversations, we can take a "beat" to stop judgmental thoughts from adversely affecting a relationship.

I'm not usually a fan of meme wisdom, but sometimes the internet gets it right:

The first thought that goes through your mind is what you have been conditioned to think. What you think next defines who you are.[27]

Delving into what you've been conditioned to think is far beyond the scope of the ACTER model. I'd like you to focus on the slight pause between what you first think and the thought that defines you. In that break, you have two choices. You can potentially shut down the conversation by being judgmental, or you can play the "why game." Why does my conversation partner feel this way? What is their background that contributed to the life they live today? What question could you ask that could help clarify your conversation partner's point that you so vehemently disagree with?

Some forms of judgment are learned behaviors used as defense mechanisms. While some protect us, some can derail a vital conversation, erode trust, and be damning to a relationship. The pause between unhealthy conditioned thinking and defining who you want to be is a chance to examine how and why you default to a judgmental position. The following are six ways the mind moves us into unhealthy judgmental defaults. Each provides insight into what they reveal about you for defaulting to it and a way to navigate back into a curious mindset. The six judgmental defaults that I commonly see creep into courageous conversations are:

1. Defining a person by a single act.
2. Expecting perfection of others.
3. Making moral evaluations.
4. Judging based on limited or imperfect knowledge.
5. Believing someone else's lifestyle has a negative impact on you.
6. Using your life experiences as a yardstick for everyone else.

## 1. Defining a Person by a Single Act

Not every little action you take represents the entirety of who you are. Think about when you were having a bad day and said something out of sheer frustration. On quick reflection, you might backpedal on your momentary lash-out by saying, "I'm sorry, I wasn't acting like myself." When you're overly judgmental of someone, you may tend to latch onto a single momentary lapse of reason or foible to define that person's character. We often see this behavior in how we view public figures like politicians or celebrities. For example, a media talking head might point out that the politician you love to hate used the wrong fork while dining with another head of state. You then use that to make the snap judgment that someone who doesn't know the difference between a salad and a table fork is too incompetent to make economic policy decisions. The truth of the matter is we are all human. We all have bad days. We all make mistakes. No one is perfect, and judging someone based on a single moment is unfair. However, if we already have a predisposed perception of a person, any action or mistake can be heightened and blown out of proportion to reinforce our beliefs.

Curiosity suspends judgment. The answer to unintentionally focusing on a single data point in a conversation is to pause your brain and emotions. Stay curious about yourself and your motivations. Here are some questions you should pose before making a snap judgment.

- Have I asked enough questions?
- Have I heard the entire story in its proper context?
- Am I making an assessment based on facts or am I reacting out of emotions?
- If I asked three different dispassionate people if my judgment was accurate, what would they say?
- What biases do I hold about this situation that I need to acknowledge?
- Am I looking for a way to support a belief I already have?
- If I examine the situation in an hour, will I feel the same way?

You should hold off on making any judgments until you have the full story. If you're having problems keeping a curious mindset during a conversation, the "Phrases of Curiosity" section at the end of the chapter will give you examples of conversation cues.

## 2. Expecting Perfection of Others

A variation of judging someone on a single act is expecting someone to execute their standards or ideas flawlessly every single time. You probably don't expect perfection in yourself, so you shouldn't expect it in others. The expectation of perfection in our conversation partners is a dangerous road. You risk your conversation partner feeling like nothing they do or say is correct in your eyes. If your conversation partner makes a mistake or says the wrong thing, and you judgmentally hold their feet to the fire, they will likely shut down and not have any more conversations with you.

A quest for perfection and spotting any defects in your conversation partner's actions often occurs when emotions are high. This tactic may be used as a defense mechanism to deflect, utilized when we do not want to agree with someone. Likely, you've entered the conversation with a win-lose or lose-lose mindset. Either you will win at all costs, or you're willing to scorch the earth beneath your own feet to prove your point and, more importantly, disprove theirs. When you see this happen, it's a good idea to pause the conversation. Take a breath and reevaluate the reason you're having the conversation in the first place. Then, you should think about baseball. Yes, I said baseball.

Think about your conversation partner as a baseball player. No one expects the player to hit every pitch every time a player goes up to bat. Professional baseball players are considered excellent if they get a hit 30 percent of the time they're at bat. A batting average of 40 percent is virtually unheard of in professional baseball.[28] If a professional ball player can be considered success-ful by "getting the batting thing right" 30 percent of the time, I'd suggest adopting the same mentality with your conversation part-ner. The person you're speaking with might have screwed up once or twice on a certain point. If your conversation partner sticks to their standards and values most of the time, you should evaluate them on their batting average. It is okay to bring a mistake to the attention of your conversation partner. However, it should not be used as a weapon against them or to judge them.

## 3. Making Moral Evaluations

One of the biggest challenges that I see creep into courageous conversations is the insertion of moral evaluations of others. Judgments along moral evaluation lines assign an arbitrary and binary view of the world—either something is good or bad. There are no gray areas, equivocations, or justifications for those mak-ing moral evaluations. You generally see moral evaluations hap-pen when someone has strict interpretations of some rulebook. Those guidelines could be anything from a religious text to a po-litical party's platform or even an employee handbook. When you use a moral judgment in a conversation, you are not showing that you want to have a conversation. You are showing that you want to use your moral compass to control, and potentially influence, the conversation and its participants.

Moral evaluations can have considerable consequences beyond courageous conversations. If you're a healthcare professional, a moral evaluation of someone's lifestyle or behavior could negatively impact and reduce the amount of care you give that patient. Real estate agents could make moral evaluations to steer homebuyers to certain neighborhoods and avoid others. *He's wearing a hoodie, so he's up to no good. If you're there at that time of night, you've got to be looking for trouble. There's something wrong with you if you're reading a book like that.* These are all moral evaluation judgments.

Moral evaluation judgments are possibly the most difficult to weed out of our thought process. These judgments are an evolutionary holdover from a time humans had to make survival judgments like, "Hey Bob, that's a saber-tooth tiger. That's a dangerous beast, and we should run." When faced with a moral evaluation, try to understand what and why you want to take control over someone else.

Let's say you see someone reading a book you heard has offensive language. You haven't picked up the book yourself, but you've been told it's bad. You believe that keeping the book away from your friend (your control method) is for their own good. You're on the cusp of making a moral judgment. Instead of making a sweeping proclamation that could damage your relationship, combat your judgment with curiosity. Try this: "I've heard some pretty racy stuff in that book. Are you okay with that type of language?" You've opened up a dialogue without slapping the book out of your friend's hands.

## 4. Judgments Based on Limited or Imperfect Knowledge

Working in the diversity and inclusion space, I love when participants realize that they have limited knowledge of the experiences of others. This can be due to a lack of exposure, proximity, or awareness. Without this awareness, they may judge others based on limited or imperfect knowledge. This brand of judgment is often closely associated with the biases that we hold. It is based on the fallacy that your limited knowledge, experience, or point of view on a topic is the only possible interpretation of a situation. You make limited knowledge judgments for a few different reasons. First, you may be trying to connect with your conversation partner by sharing your experience. Often, this approach could do more harm than good in a conversation. Your conversation partner can see you as not having any interest in what they have to say because you've already got everything figured out. Consider this conversation:

"I am so shaken up. I got pulled over by the police on the way here."

"Why are you so shaken up? That's not a big deal. I get pulled over all the time. Just do what they say, and it will be fine."

Sharing the above reaction from their frame of reference wasn't productive for anyone. Let's quickly analyze this. The person who shared that they got pulled over actually never asked for help or advice. They shared their experience and how it made them feel. Yet, the other person responded with more information than necessary, which wasn't even relevant to the initial statement. Influential author and educator Brené Brown addresses this in her book *Atlas of the Heart.*

> We need to dispel the myth that empathy is walking in someone else's shoes. Rather than walking in your shoes, I need to learn how to listen to the story you tell about what it's like in your shoes and believe you even when it doesn't match my experiences.[29]

Brown's advice sounds like a no-brainer, but courageous conversations take on a different dynamic where diverse lived experiences are involved.

You may not have experienced what your conversation partner has, or even know anything about it. Some courageous conversations require you to step outside your perspective and listen to your conversation partner's experience. Be curious and ask questions. Understand why something made a person feel the way that it did, even if that's not how you would have responded emotionally. This is sometimes challenging. It is often easier to deflect than dive into life's hard circumstances. Even when you feel you are on shaky intellectual or emotional ground, be vulnerable enough to remain curious. It is okay to say that you don't know much about the topic and ask your conversation partner for context. Everyone cannot know everything, and exhibiting curiosity about a topic you don't know about can strengthen a relationship. Sometimes we have to ask ourselves if we are speaking to be smart or curious.

## 5. Believing Someone Else's Lifestyle Has a Negative Impact on You

You're driving home from work one day and notice that a couple of streets over, one of your neighbors painted a mural on the side of her house. You can't see the mural from your home. The mural isn't in violation of any city ordinance. The artwork doesn't depict anything obscene or violent. You can even take another way home from work and never have to see the mural ever again, but something about it rubs you the wrong way. You don't like the style of art. The colors aren't right. The mural is just downright tacky. Based on these factors, you make the judgment call that your neighborhood is destined to go to hell in a handbasket. As a result, you feel a moral obligation to intervene. If you don't stop this, what else could it lead to?

When we make these judgments, we expose an irrational fear of losing something. In the case of the mural, your judgment is that the house art will drive property values down or create an undefined nuance that will negatively impact you. When you come up against this line of judgment, think about how your life has changed since the mural was painted. If your evaluation is honest, having a mural in your neighborhood probably didn't change a thing. You go about your life the same. Your relationships with your friends and loved ones haven't been impacted, and more than likely won't be. We must remind ourselves that everyone has agency over their decisions and how they live their lives. It is okay to choose not to live as another person does, but we must be mindful when our choices become judgments of others. In those moments, look at the situation through an analytical lens and evaluate the true impact another person's decisions or lifestyle will have on your life.

## 6. Using Your Life's Experience as a Yardstick for Everyone Else

Over the last ten years, I've seen a sharp rise in this type of judgment in intergenerational conversations. I think of this judgment when a baby boomer or Generation Xer comments to a millennial or Generation Z, "I worked my way through college without debt, so why can't you?" This judgment comes from the flawed assumption that everyone's circumstances are identical. I can assure you that someone who grew up right next door to you doesn't have all the same experiences that you do. You might be best friends with the person next door and never know their whole story. If that's the case, don't expect that everyone has the same advantages or disadvantages you had.

If you start any sentence with, "Back in my day ..." stop yourself. The curious approach to navigating this judgment is to ask what challenges your conversation partner is facing. Try not to couple your curiosity here with an armchair quarterback mentality. Being curious about someone's circumstances doesn't help much if you're going to criticize your conversation partner for what you perceive as poor decisions. As with trying to ward off any judgment, let this be your guide:

- Stop for a moment.
- Ask a question to help you understand your conversation partner's point of view.
- Don't say a word—simply listen.
- If what they've said to you doesn't make sense, ask follow-up questions or hush up until you can think of something nice to say.

## How to Engage with Curiosity

Now that we've outlined a strategy to quash judgments, it's time to learn how to be curious. Engaging your conversation partner with curiosity isn't as easy as the "why game," but it's not much more complicated. You must practice curiosity to the point it becomes second nature. If you're an extrovert, you likely practice many aspects of engaging with interest without thinking twice about it. That doesn't mean you can skip this section. Your natural talent for engaging others in conversation can continuously be refined. For introverts curled up reading on their couches, I have identified that being curious during a courageous conversation may be more difficult. My best suggestion for you is simple—practice. Like anything in life, building your confidence and competence takes practice. The more you intentionally start and engage in rich dialogues with people from diverse backgrounds and perspectives, the more comfortable you'll learn to become talking about anything. Also, luckily for you introverts, the first step of engaging with curiosity is silence.

A courageous conversation aims to engage in a dialogue where we expand our perspectives. To do that, we must engage in vulnerability, share with our conversation partner the lived experiences that shaped our perspectives, and be equally willing to hear their experiences. This approach humanizes the dialogue and is grounded in curiosity. However, before we can exhibit curiosity about anyone else, we must first trust that they are not misrepresenting their experiences, and that they are being honest.

When two people feel strongly about opposing viewpoints, human nature dictates that they each become suspicious of everything the other person says during that conversation. We assume that our conversation partner is attempting to use any means necessary to woo us away from our position. But unless you have seen moments where your conversation partner has been manipulative and deceitful, you should approach it with the mindset that they will probably not be disingenuous about what their life is like or why they feel the way they feel.

Trust is a massive component of a courageous conversation. When you trust your conversation partner is expressing their point of view accurately, you can focus on the content of what they're saying. What can you learn from your conversation partner's perspective? Can your conversation partner teach you something about a topic you know little about? Are there parts of what your conversation partner is saying that you want a more in-depth discussion of? These are the fruits of coupling trust with curiosity.

Now the question is, what if you find yourself in a courageous conversation with someone whom you do not know, and there is minimal trust? In this case, I recommend proceeding with caution and curiosity. This means listening to gather information more than speaking. Suppose it is a courageous conversation with someone you have little trust in because of past encounters. You may want to consider making your courageous conversation focused on addressing the issues of trust.

Being curious also means just that: simply being curious for the sake of gaining more understanding of a topic or issue. Pure curiosity means listening to understand and not feeling that you always have to share your point of view. It is less talking and more engaging genuinely through questions and observation to learn, grow, and understand. Curiosity is not about right or wrong. There is no cosmic rule that says, "If I don't agree with someone, they must know exactly how I feel about it." It is simply a personal exploration for creating a deeper understanding and broadened perspective around a topic. It allows for expansive thinking. This means that even on topics where we have strongly divergent views, we still can and should engage in curiosity to learn as much as possible about the topic. Pure curiosity is the fact-finding of information. Whether the information we garner affirms or even invalidates our assumptions, we are open to it because it allows for critical thinking and a broadened perspective. To be curious, we must permanently remove a sense of moral obligation to let someone know why they're wrong and why you're right about an issue. When we do that, we are engaging in judgment. That is important to be aware of because judgment blocks curiosity.

The mind cannot both be in judgment and curiosity at the same time. Many courageous conversations happen because two people trying to solve a mutual problem find common ground with each other to achieve a goal or discuss a different point of view. The seas will not dry up, and mountains will not crumble if you enter and exit a conversation without explaining your point of view to your conversation partner. Let's see how the need to share a point of view versus being curious plays out with two coworkers, Anne and Jim. This exchange is incredibly uncomfortable, but it shows how damaging the need to share our perspectives can be in a courageous conversation.

"I heard that those two fresh-out-of-college kids they hired got a full minority scholarship at State. What's up with that?" asked Anne.

"Minority scholarships are to provide kids with disadvantages in life an opportunity to go to college," said Jim.

"I don't think that's right. Everyone should have an equal opportunity at scholarships. No one gave me a scholarship because I'm Irish," replied Anne.

"You know I'm Black and had a full scholarship to the same school?" asked Jim.

"I know that. It doesn't make it right that you got a scholarship just because of the color of your skin," said Anne.

While these may be Anne's views, her responses have effectively shut down any further conversation between the two—ever. I think it is fair to say that any possibility of a cordial relationship has been eliminated. Imagine how difficult it would be for Jim to communicate with Anne. Think how the conversation would have been different if Anne didn't feel the need to assert her perspective in that manner. Once Jim advised her about why minority scholarships exist, a simple "Thanks for letting me know" would have been a pleasant way to end the conversation without turning it into a confrontation. A curious and open-minded approach could have been for Anne to ask Jim what disadvantages minority students face and why it's important that persons of color have access to college.

There's a misconception that being open-minded equates to changing your beliefs or value sets. Nothing could be further from the truth. Being open-minded means that you're willing to listen to different and opposing viewpoints. When someone truly listens to an opposing viewpoint with an open mind, our perceptions have an opportunity to change and be expanded through this additional knowledge. But listening to what someone else says doesn't ever mean you are giving up on a firmly held belief. Listening, in this instance, doesn't mean letting someone else speak. Listening in this context means hearing and digesting what someone else is saying. We'll discuss active listening techniques in this book's "Respectful Listening" chapter. Now, know that having an open mind and asking open-ended questions does not negate your opinions.

When you ask open-ended questions, you maximize your chances of finding out more about your conversation partner. Consider how these two questions are framed:

"Did you have a good day at work?"
"What happened at work today?"

The first question is considered a closed question because it elicits a simple, direct response of one or a few words. The second question is regarded as open-ended because the answer requires more information. When we ask open-ended questions, we signal to our conversation partners that we are interested and invested in their responses.

## Phrases of Curiosity

If you become mindful of asking open-ended questions, these questions will become second nature to you. But sometimes, you're in a conversation and get stumped. Your conversation partner just said something that makes zero sense, and you don't know what to say. These phrases are suggestions and, of course, need to be used in the proper context. You can use these phrases to combat judgmental behaviors and cultivate a curious mindset during your conversation.

- Can you help me understand what you just said?
- How does that work?
- I'm not familiar with that. Could you please share more about that with me?
- It is always interesting to hear different perspectives on this very important topic. Would you mind sharing more of your thoughts?
- Tell me about your experiences with_____.
- Tell me more about that.
- That is very interesting. Could you please share your thought process with me?
- What benefits are there for doing it this way?

- What else?
- While that has not been my experience, I am interested in your perspective.

If none of those phrases fit, there is one "break-glass-in-case-of-emergency" tactic—the "last-three-words" trick. I've had clients who aren't sports fans use this in situations where they become involved in sports ball talk. The strategy is to phrase the last three words someone says differently to keep the conversation going. Here's an example:

"In the second half, what was the ref thinking?"
"Dude, I can't imagine what the ref was thinking!"
"Smith was offside, and he missed it."
"How did he miss it?"

You can keep a conversation going nearly indefinitely using the last-three-words tactic, but you should use this sparingly. Your conversation partner will pick up on your actions, and you'll seem disingenuous. Only use the last-three-words tactic if you are out of options and need a moment to regain your conversational footing.

Memorizing phrases or using the last-three-words tactic is simply a way to cultivate curiosity within a conversation. What you cannot remember is being authentically interested in what your conversation partner has to say. A courageous conversation is not a "fake it 'til you make it" proposition. You're more likely to do more harm than good if your conversation partner believes you to be disingenuous. It's better to say: "I'm not in the right frame of mind for this conversation right now. Can we talk when I can give you the attention this conversation deserves?" than throw out canned phrases to feign curiosity.

## Putting It All Together

As with all the components that make up the ACTER model, the goal is to expose you to new ways of thinking. Incorporating curiosity as a mindset and eliminating judgment types won't immediately take root in your conversational habits. Every new skill set takes time to master, so give yourself grace if you don't believe you were as curious as you thought you should be in your next conversation. Start using your curiosity skills in conversations that don't require courage first. Let's say you're talking to a friend about a movie they have seen, but you have not. Use this opportunity to practice your curiosity skills and dig deeper into what your friend thought about the film than, "Yeah, it was okay." Here are a few examples of how you can practice being curious in a casual movie conversation:

"Who starred in that film? Have you seen any of their other movies?"

"Wasn't that set in the 1960s? Do you think it was true to the era?"

"Is this movie family-friendly? My son wants to see it, but I'm not sure it's age-appropriate for him."

Each of these questions builds a dialogue and trust between you and your movie-watching friend. Most importantly, you are interested in your conversation partner's thoughts and feelings. Remember, you should go into any courageous conversation wanting to learn about your conversation partner. You may have strong feelings about the topic you're discussing, but not every conversation has to be about your point of view. If you're patient and show that you're curious about your conversation partner, I promise they will be curious about you too.

We all have emotional baggage from our past that we bring into courageous conversations. If you get flustered in the middle of a conversation, stop and reflect on the rules and strategies. Give yourself a moment and take a breath. Be curious about yourself and your conversation partner. Ask yourself, "What are you feeling and why are you feeling this way?" Then think, "How would I like my conversation partner to express their curiosity about me?" After you answer that question, implement how you'd like to be treated. Recognizing how you'd like to be treated in a conversation will play a large part in the ACTER model's next step—triggers. Being curious about what you and your conversation partner's triggers are will make a huge difference in the outcome of any conversation.

# Chapter 3—Exercises and Examples: Curiosity

## Exercise: The Curiosity Worksheet

The Curiosity Worksheet is an exercise that works best when you're preparing for or have just concluded a courageous conversation. The goal here is not to use this as a cheat sheet while you are having a conversation—that would be incredibly awkward. Instead, use the worksheet to frame how you should think about curiosity during a conversation you will have in the future. Or, if you've just had a courageous conversation, you can use this worksheet as a review of how you utilized curiosity during the conversation. In either case, the more you review this worksheet in real-world settings, the more curious you'll become during future conversations.

Don't forget to get uncomfortable and remember to appreciate diversity of opinions. This is not an exercise in persuasion or influence, but rather in expanding our perspective and understanding. Curiosity allows us the opportunity to suspend our judgment and connect with one another on a human level. You should adopt a beginner's mindset to any conversation topic; don't assume you know everything about the topic at hand. Even if you do have foreknowledge of a topic, remember that how facts are interpreted and applied can be as important as by-the-book knowledge. If you keep a curious mind, you'll be able to challenge your assumptions on a topic. Now, on to the worksheet!

## Overview

- What is the topic of the conversation?
- What do you hope to learn from this conversation?

## Curiosity of Self

- What are my thoughts/needs on this topic? Why?
- Do I hold any concerns or fears around this topic? What are they? Why?
- Are there any triggers or trauma associated with this topic that may increase my sensitivities? What are they?
- How am I feeling at this moment (tired, hungry, busy, etc.)? Am I in the right mood and mental space to have this conversation right now?
- Why is my passion level where it is about this topic?
- What is it that I really want the other person to understand about how I feel about this topic?

## Curiosity of the Other Person

- What are their thoughts or needs on this topic? Why?
- Does the other person possibly hold any concerns or fears around this topic? What might they be? Why?
- Do they come to this conversation with any possible triggers or trauma associated with the topic that may increase their sensitivities? What might they be? (If you're unsure of the answer to this, read the next chapter, "Triggers," to help you understand what your conversation partner may be going through.)
- How might they be feeling at this moment (tired, hungry, busy, etc.)? Are they in the right mood and mental space to have this conversation right now?
- Why is their passion level where it is about this topic?
- What is it that the other person may really want me to understand about how they feel about this topic?

## *Examples*

### What Do You Want for Dinner?

Early in their relationship, the "what do you want to have for dinner" discussion was fun for John and Dani. The couple had different enough tastes that choosing a dinner location was a mini adventure. As their time together passed, the thought of choosing a restaurant for dinner became as much fun as doing taxes. John wasn't sure what the problem was. Whenever one of them threw out a suggestion, the other threw up the "I don't care what we choose, but let's not go there" wall.

As silly as it sounds, dinner plan indifference was becoming such a sore subject in their relationship. They had nearly stopped going out to eat altogether. Tonight, date night was John's responsibility, and he didn't feel like cooking. He called up Dani with a plan to approach the dinner conundrum with curiosity.

"I have an idea for dinner tonight. Let's go to that Ethiopian place over on Signal Street," said John, hoping his suggestion would float.

"Eh ... can we go somewhere else?" asked Dani.

"I thought you liked Ethiopian. Can you help me understand why that's a bad choice?" asked John.

"I saw something online last week that they didn't do too well on their health inspection," said Dani.

*At least that's a valid reason*, thought John. He replied, "I didn't know that, or I wouldn't have suggested it. Did you see somewhere that scored well on the health inspector's list that you might want to try?"

"There was a Korean place on Third Avenue that was on the list. I looked them up. They had good reviews, too," said Dani.

"I'm not familiar with that place. Could you please share more about that with me?" asked John.

Dani went on to describe the menu and the customer comments that she'd read. John liked what he was hearing, and it looked like date night would come with a serving of kimchi and glass noodles.

Using the tools of curiosity, John found out that reviews and health department scores were important decision-making tools for Dani. Now on future date nights, he knew that if he did a little background research before making a dinner suggestion, the process might go smoother. Curiosity gives us the groundwork for understanding. Understanding gives us ways to make meaningful decisions and compromises that can show pathways forward and improve our relationships!

**Hey, That's My Spreadsheet!**

Mija was steamed. For the last six weeks, she'd developed an integrated spreadsheet that pulled several individual resources together in one place. She'd tinkered with the spreadsheet's design over the last few months, stealing a few minutes before a meeting here and a little time during a video meeting there. Two weeks ago, Mija's masterpiece was complete. During the first week, Mija decided to integrate the spreadsheet's functionality into her workflow. Aside from a few minor tweaks, it worked like a charm.

Now it was time to see if someone else would think the spreadsheet was helpful. Mija chose Aaron to be her test subject. Aaron was relatively new to the company, and Mija wanted a fresh set of eyes on her work before presenting it to her boss. First thing Monday morning, Mija showed Aaron her spreadsheet, but didn't tell him how hard she'd worked on it. She wanted honest feedback without Aaron feeling like he had to say something nice about the work. All Mija asked was for Aaron to let her know if the spreadsheet was useful at the end of the week.

By Wednesday, the department was abuzz about how Aaron, the new guy, had created this killer spreadsheet that was going to save everyone hours of work. Mija's first inclination was to jump to the conclusion that Aaron had distributed the spreadsheet to department members in a bid to make a good early impression. She considered ratting Aaron out to her boss for stealing her work. That would surely put him in his place. Instead, Mija decided to be curious instead of jumping to conclusions. Here's how their conversation went:

"Hey, Aaron. What was your experience with that spreadsheet?"

"I was going to get with you on Friday like you asked. I've got a few suggestions, but overall, it worked great," said Aaron.

"Can you walk me though your thought processes on sharing it with the rest of the team?" asked Mija.

"Anna came into my cube Tuesday morning and saw me using it. I guess I went on and on about what a great tool it was, and she asked me to forward it to her. Was I not supposed to do that? I thought the spreadsheet would help everyone out," replied Aaron.

This example shows us how curiosity defeats making unwarranted judgments. By applying curiosity, Mija sidestepped a situation with her boss that would have resulted in egg on her face. Furthermore, had Mija not approached this situation with curiosity, she could have damaged her relationship with a new coworker.

## CHAPTER 4

# T—Triggers

Up to this point in the ACTER Model, we have focused on increasing your awareness of your perspective. In Appreciating Diversity of Opinions, we analyzed how open you are to different points of view. In Chapter 3, we took you on a process to engage through curiosity. As you can tell, the ACTER Model focuses on self to improve your confidence and competence in having courageous conversations with others. As we have shown, these conversations require a heightened self-awareness as a means to self-regulate and have fruitful dialogue. I tell my clients that you cannot regulate what you are unaware of.

That brings us to T—Triggers. Creating a culture that encourages engaging in courageous conversation drives innovation, creativity, mutual trust, and more prosperous relationships. As a result, many of my clients are corporations and governmental entities. Since the unfortunate death of George Floyd, several of my clients have required their employees to attend my sessions with the goal of cultivating the essential competencies to have courageous conversations. This creates a dynamic where I know a certain percentage of the participants may not necessarily want to be there or are uncertain about exactly why the training is even necessary.

In sessions where I guide participants through the ACTER model, I usually get people who began skeptically to quickly buy in while discussing appreciating diverse opinions and curiosity. Even hardcore cynics understand the value of listening to others and asking thoughtful questions. This attitude of openness can sometimes change when I get to T in the ACTER model—the trigger section. When I get to triggers, some participants get a bit uncomfortable. Over the years, I have identified a negative connotation with the word "trigger." It is often misused as an expression when someone is opposed to a position or feels offended about something. It is also weaponized and used in a derogatory sense to mock someone's emotional reaction to a situation. The word and its meaning have been watered down to be associated with minor moments of sadness or disgust or as an insult to people who are perceived as overly sensitive.

I think it is necessary to dispel some myths about triggers and being triggered. As we will see, the stimulus and response interaction that causes triggering is usually related to some past trauma or an unresolved negative experience. Like all steps in the ACTER model, triggers are an apolitical concept grounded in science, theory, and research. As we reference triggers, it is not a psychological tactic used to manipulate or advance a political agenda or ideology. Emotional triggers are real. Being triggered is part of the human experience and happens regardless of race, creed, or sexual orientation.

Being triggered is also not a sign of weakness or something you should ignore in yourself or someone else. Think of it like you've been sitting in a dark room and then walk outside on a sunny day. The bright light of the sun can hurt your eyes, and your automatic response is to shield your eyes. That's a stimulus (bright light) and response (covering your eyes) interaction. Whether you're a triathlete or an Olympic bodybuilder, your response to the sunlight trigger is the same as everyone else's. Also, by not properly reacting to the bright light by shielding your eyes, you risk damaging your eyesight.

As mentioned earlier, being triggered is not analogous to being offended by what your conversation partner has to say. Being offended is when someone finds another person's statement objectionable. Let's say that Alice is wearing a crop top, and someone jokingly says, "Aren't you a little too fluffy for clothes like that?" That is a crappy thing to say to someone and is likely to cause Alice to be offended. Being offended by an off-the-cuff statement isn't the same as being triggered. Here's where it gets tricky. That same statement can also be a trigger if it dredges up a reaction to past trauma. If Alice grew up with a parent who constantly body-shamed her and berated her about her weight and how she looked in clothes, that statement could also be emotionally triggering for her. In other words, one can be offended *and* emotionally triggered by the same statement. The difference is the deep emotional attachment that you have to the comment based on your life experiences and traumas.

If you feel like comprehending triggers is a bit complicated, you'd be absolutely correct. Triggers are possibly the most challenging concept of the ACTER model to understand and implement because it asks you to identify and understand subconscious emotional responses to hurtful past events. That's in dealing with the triggers you have. Many of us are unaware of our triggers. Without intentionally analyzing ourselves and understanding what from our past creates high emotional responses, you are basically walking into a land mine blindfolded, and our emotional responses are the bombs hidden in the ground, ready to explode. Imagine the impact of this unknown on your courageous conversation. How do we untie this colossal knot of reactions to triggers? We start with examining the reality of what emotional triggers are and what being triggered means. We then learn how to identify past traumas and how they trigger us, and finally, we learn how to react kindly to emotional triggers we see surface in our conversation partners.

The key to a fruitful courageous conversation is self-regulation. In EI, self-regulation is controlling or redirecting disruptive behaviors, impulses, and moods. The first component of EI is self-awareness, followed by self-regulation, which we will discuss in the next chapter. The order of these two is imperative because you cannot regulate what you are unaware of. Because courageous conversations are grounded in divergent opinions, it is obvious that emotions are a part of the dialogue. Emotions are valuable tools for showing empathy, surprise, and even passion. However, when our emotions take control of us, we can find ourselves derailing an important conversation and potentially ruining a relationship. Our previous focus on self-awareness was a tee-up to assist us in our ability to self-regulate. In this chapter, I will walk you through a process where you can proactively identify your triggers to minimize the impact they have on you and your responses during courageous conversations.

This chapter aims to introduce you to a healthy examination of emotional triggers and how to keep your courageous conversation on track despite triggers. For this step of the ACTER model, you'll be guided through ways to identify and create strategies to regulate triggers during a courageous conversation. Think of this process in terms of Marvel's Dr. Bruce Banner/the Hulk. When Dr. Banner gets angry (triggered), he turns into a muscle-bound green monstrosity prone to smashing everything in sight. The Hulk's challenge was his inability to manage his transformation. This chapter should give you the tools to gain control of your emotions and avoid having your triggers become your version of the Hulk destroying your courageous conversation.

## What Is a Trigger?

The easiest way to understand triggers is to take the concept to its base level. Previously we noted that a trigger is a stimulus and emotional response event. Let's see how that works in a setting you're likely familiar with. You probably know that scents are more closely linked to memories and emotions than any of your other senses[30]. Have you ever walked through a store and smelled a perfume or cologne that reminded you of someone? Maybe catching a whiff of freshly baked cookies reminds you of your childhood, when you used to spend holidays baking with your grandmother. In each of these examples, the scent is the trigger that evokes a memory.

Emotional triggers are more nuanced than memory triggers of perfumes and nostalgia. The triggers we'll discuss in this chapter are topics, phrases, events, or circumstances that produce uncomfortable emotional responses such as anxiety, frustration, panic, or discomfort. Certainly, not all emotional triggers associated with memories are harmful, like the previous perfume and cookie examples. However, having pleasant memory triggers generally won't elicit unpleasant emotions or derail a courageous conversation. So, for this step in the ACTER model, we use the term *trigger* to denote only adverse emotional reactions that we experience.

Let's look at how emotional triggers arise. A participant in one of my classes, Paul, shared an emotional trigger: his mother. Paul is an openly gay man. He spoke about feeling that he has never really been able to talk to his mother about his love life without being triggered. Paul shared that when he came out to his parents, his mother initially seemed supportive. Sixteen years later, when Paul had conversations about his personal life with his mother, he always felt a level of irritation and frustration that he could never explain. Paul's mother would always listen to Paul talk about going on dates, but she was never fully present in the conversations or interested in Paul's life. Often, she would offer a platitude about Paul's story and quickly try to change the subject to something else.

Paul told himself that while his mother loves and supports him, she is from an older generation and simply could not connect with him. Over time Paul chose to share less and less about his love life with his mother. While that felt like the safest option to Paul, the ramifications were a shallow relationship between the two of them. After working closely with Paul one-on-one, we were able to pin down the exact events that caused him to become emotionally triggered. When his mother spoke with Paul, she often used the word *choice* when discussing his life. You may think that's a simple word, but to Paul it meant everything. Whenever his mother said *choice* when speaking about his sexual orientation, he felt that his identity was being questioned and he would become emotionally triggered. This revelation was powerful for Paul. The word *choice* made Paul feel that his mother believed that he was choosing to be gay versus accepting it as his true identity. Such a seemingly small thing had been creating a high emotional response and driven a wedge between him and his mother.

# There is No Trigger without a Trauma, and Trauma Isn't What You Think It Is

It's easy to miss the plot when dealing with triggers. In Paul's case, you can get lost in the trigger being a single word. The trauma for Paul was wrapped up in everyone questioning his identity and equating it to a choice. I'm sure some of those comments were hurtful and came from a place of prejudice. When Paul's mother, who tried to be a safe place for Paul, used the word *choice*, it brought back all of those other traumatic statements to Paul's mind. Paul had to be curious about himself to determine why he was being triggered and what trauma was behind it. What was behind it was a feeling of rejection.

We're often quick to dismiss our triggers because we don't believe the underlying trauma is severe enough to warrant a reaction. Let's say the last time you felt triggered was when your conversation partner was constantly looking at their phone. You felt that what you had to say was trivial if your conversation partner could not give you their full attention. To express your frustrations, you made a snarky comment about never being taken seriously that derailed any further fruitful conversation. The only thing you accomplished was getting you and your conversation partner riled up, and the resolution to your courageous conversation will have to wait for another day.

After the conversation's conclusion, the next step is to be curious about yourself in order to understand why your conversation partner's actions made you uncomfortable. So, you do something insanely difficult—sit in a quiet room and do some self-examination. You try to think of all the times you've felt ignored during your life, starting with your earliest memories and working forward. You guessed there was one grand event that would explain why feeling ignored gets you torqued up, but there's not. You can only see a pattern of more minor incidents that make you feel invisible. You are reminded that your upbringing wasn't like a kid on a TV sitcom. You were an only child with an emotionally distant mother who spent more time shopping than with you. Your father continued to read his newspaper while you told him about your day at school. Compounding the situation were the times in college when you weren't invited to parties because you weren't the right fit for the crowd. You threw out an idea in all those work meetings and were dismissed because you were just a junior associate. You feel that maybe none of these instances, taken by themselves, is worthy of being triggered, and your hour-long walk down memory lane was useless.

The truth is that you uncovered the trauma behind your trigger. Instead of acknowledging the trauma for what it is, you've diminished the impact of that trauma on your life. Sometimes we don't recognize trauma, and its associated triggers, because we don't see them as being "that bad." How could you possibly be triggered in a conversation with your significant other today when your dad wouldn't listen to you as a kid? It happens.

Let's start with some baseline definitions of trauma. Emotional trauma results from experiences that leave one feeling unsafe and often helpless.[31] That trauma can be anything from living through a tornado to being ignored by a loved one. If you ignore the root traumas in your lives, no matter how insignificant they might seem, you'll never be able to deal with the triggers associated with them. Think of minor traumas like stepping on a rusty nail. The wound itself might not look that bad or even hurt too much. However, if you haven't gotten a tetanus shot in the last few years, you could get lockjaw and die. You have to attend to the trauma. Frequently, we choose emotional suppression and ignore the trauma. However, the emotion associated with trauma is like trash: if you keep sweeping it under the rug, you are bound to trip over it one day. Feelings associated with trauma do not go away. And the unfortunate part is, if not dealt with, they usually surface and show themselves when we least expect it.

My rule is that if a trauma is bad enough to alter your behavior (being triggered), then that trauma is worth examining. Unfortunately, the scope of this book doesn't extend to how to heal from your past emotional traumas. Suppose you have unresolved traumas that are affecting your behavior. In that case, I strongly suggest you speak to a mental health professional, research strategies to address your trauma, or attend a support group.[32] Whether you take those steps or not, you'll still have to identify sources of trauma that trigger you. If you don't know how to start looking for past traumas, here are some common conversation trauma-inducing areas:

- Being ignored or invalidated
- Betrayal
- Challenged beliefs
- Disapproval or criticism
- Feeling disrespected
- Raised voice or yelling
- Feeling unwanted or unneeded
- Demands
- Manipulation
- Feeling of loss of independence or controlled
- Rejection or judgment
- Feeling scolded or blamed
- Unfair /unbalanced or double standard
- Feeling unheard

In all the talk of trauma and triggers, it's easy to lose sight of what our goal in this chapter is—to understand what triggers you and create strategies to avoid having your triggers sabotage your courageous conversations. Once you've identified the areas of trauma in your life, it gives you a leg up on understanding how those traumas will trigger you. In our previous example of feeling ignored during a courageous conversation, the trigger for feeling ignored was your conversation partner looking at their cell phone. Your conversation partner could have just as easily been walking around the room, washing dishes, or acting in any other way that would make you feel like your message was not worth their attention. Any of these actions could have caused the trigger of feeling ignored. However, suppose you know that there's trauma associated with being ignored. In that case, you can proactively look for behaviors, words, or phrases from your conversation partner that could trigger you. This self-awareness gives us great power and control over our emotions. Instead of reactively saying something hurtful to your conversation partner, you could recognize the trigger and politely ask them to put away their cell phone because it makes you feel like the conversation isn't important to them.

## Does Having Triggers Mean I've Got PTSD?

Earlier, we mentioned that one of the issues in discussing triggers is that the concept is trivialized or mythologized. The other end of that spectrum is the misconception that if someone has a trigger, that means they have post-traumatic stress disorder (PTSD). According to the American Psychiatric Association, PTSD is a:

> ... psychiatric disorder [that] may occur in people who
> have experienced or witnessed a traumatic event,

series of events, or a set of circumstances. An individual may experience this as emotionally or physically harmful or life-threatening, affecting mental, physical, social, and/or spiritual well-being. Examples include natural disasters, serious accidents, terrorist acts, war/combat, rape/sexual assault, historical trauma, intimate partner violence, and bullying.[33]

PTSD can be a debilitating disorder. We commonly hear PTSD associated with our combat veteran population. Some veterans struggle to reintegrate into civilian society when they return from service because of PTSD. Everything from cars backfiring to someone at the grocery store saying the wrong thing may trigger a flashback to the combat zone. Up to 20 percent of combat veterans exhibit some form of PTSD. [34]

While we are familiar with PTSD in combat veterans, PTSD can occur in anyone. As the definition above states, any severe trauma can cause PTSD. While triggers are a key part of PTSD, this book will not address the psychiatric disorder. Having emotional triggers often does not mean you have PTSD. Again, everyone has triggers. However, if you see severe negative patterns of behavior in your life that can be directly linked to your triggers, you should speak with a mental health professional. Also, know that feeling triggered is a normal aspect of being human, and you're not alone.

## How Do I Know if I'm Being Triggered?

When trying to identify traumas and triggers, you're up against a "which came first, the chicken or the egg" situation. If you've never been introspective enough to assess past traumas, how can you possibly know what triggers you? Conversely, if you aren't sure how you respond to triggers, how could you figure out the base trauma? There's a direct path to cracking this particular nut. Some traumas and their triggers will become apparent to you simply through introspection. The more elusive traumas must be sorted out after you've been triggered. For that to happen, you'll need to know what being triggered is like.

Triggers create a flight, fight, or freeze reaction within us.[35] Our minds perceive the trigger as something that will cause us pain and take appropriate physiological action to protect ourselves. That defensive response is highly individualized, but the following four categories are where most people will see how being triggered will affect them.

## Mentally

If a topic, phrase, event, or circumstance causes you to immediately get flustered and lose or negatively change your train of thought, you should take immediate notice. Your mind is throwing up a wall to whatever is happening around you and forcing you to focus on the trigger. Sometimes this mental defense takes the form of negative thought patterns. You might fall into a "why bother" mindset when triggered. This is when you feel that your words or actions will no longer change the outcome of a situation, so why bother to act or speak up? Worst-case scenario thinking could also kick in. The trigger could inexplicably force you into thinking about horrible consequences that are now about to happen. You could also feel like the victim and blame your present circumstances on anyone or anything other than yourself.

There are thousands of ways your mind can try to protect itself after being triggered. Simply being aware of the point the defensive switch flips in your mind can be enough to guard against the trigger. If you can, as soon as you identity that your thinking has changed, objectively ask yourself why this happened. You'll likely not get an answer immediately, and don't feel bad if you don't. Make a note of what was going on around you, the conversation topic, and what your conversation partner just said. After the conversation is over, go back and examine what could have triggered you.

If you're in the middle of a courageous conversation and find that the mental defense is too distracting, there's nothing wrong with pausing the conversation or concluding it until you've calmed down some. It's much better to say, "Can we please take a few minutes and come back to this?" than to say something reactionary that will damage a relationship.

## Physically

Since all triggers activate the fight, flight, or freeze response in us, there are physiological reactions that go along with that response. Your body is literally preparing itself for combat. The heart will start beating faster to over-oxygenate your blood. Your face may become red and flush with the extra blood flow. You may clench your teeth or your neck may tighten. You may start to sweat even though you aren't involved in physical activity. Some triggers may cause you to feel numb or disassociate, like the events around you are happening to someone else. Unless you have a medical condition that causes any of these changes, take notice because you may have been triggered.

Generally, the physical effects of a trigger cannot be avoided or controlled. There are breathing techniques that can help with slowing your heart rate, but that takes practice and patience to master. Even if you are successful with calming certain physical effects of being triggered, you're not going to be able to control the production of hormones like cortisol, histamines, and adrenalin and their effects on your body. The best you can hope for is to ride out the storm of physical effects. The only consolation is that the next time you get dry mouth or a tight chest after being triggered, you can start to figure out what trauma caused those physical effects and collect them as data points to be mindful of.

## Emotionally

I've separated out mental and emotional responses in this list because we must think of each as a separate process. Our mental process is the cold, calculating mechanics of thought and decision-making. An emotional reaction isn't the disruption of the faculties we use to solve a math problem or deciding on this year's insurance plan. When a trigger hits your emotional core, you may turn back into a moody teenager whose feelings are inexplicably all over the place. The trigger changes your sunny disposition into one of gloom and despair. You could feel suddenly anxious, agitated, or overwhelmed because of a trigger.

Whatever you're feeling because of the trigger is valid, but it's not necessarily true. For example, if you have ever been in a bad car accident and the sight of a day-old wreck on the side of the road makes you feel frightened. The feeling of anxiety itself is 100 percent valid. You were in a stressful situation that may have caused you bodily harm. However, the feeling of being in immediate danger is not true. You are in no more or less danger five minutes before seeing the wreck than you are five minutes after seeing the wreck. The trigger is making you feel something from your past that does not change the reality of your present.

102

If you're in the middle of a courageous conversation and get hit sideways with the emotional effect of a trigger, you'd do well to ask yourself, "Am I feeling this because of something my conversation partner said, or is this me feeling the effects of a past trauma?" The answer could be both. Looking back on the earlier example about feeling ignored, if your conversation partner triggers an emotion stemming from your past, that is valuable data for you to collect. However, it is important to remember to be kind to yourself. Sometimes your emotions will run so high that you won't be able to ask, or answer, that question. In either case, hit the pause button on the conversation until you gain your composure. If you feel comfortable with sharing your feelings with your conversation partner, do. Unresolved issues, over time, only turn into resentment. Honesty and candor with your conversation partner are always better options than avoidance and emotional suppression.

**Verbally**

What you say next is the final, and possibly the most indicative, reaction you can have after being triggered. The previous three responses to being triggered are all internalized. While you might have your thought patterns disrupted or get the flop sweats during a courageous conversation, these reactions will not overtly affect your conversation. At its extreme, triggers can cause us to speak out of character. From the wise words of Benjamin Franklin, "Remember not only to say the right thing in the right place, but far more difficult still, to leave unsaid the wrong thing at the tempting moment."[36] Once we say something, there's no way to take it back. You might not have meant what you just said, but saying something is a condition that will always be. You can mitigate the damage of your words, but for good or ill you are accountable for your speech.

Usually, when triggers manifest through speech you make statements like:

"You always do that."
"You never do anything I ask."
"Why are you never there for me?"
"Why don't you take a moment to understand what I'm feeling?"

Declarations like this on the heels of being triggered are rarely completely true or false. The statements are a temporary solution from your subconscious to push away your conversation partner. If the person who triggered you isn't around, they can't hurt you. While a wonderful solution for the fifteen seconds after you've hacked off your conversation partner, statements designed to keep others at arm's length aren't wonderful long-term solutions.

The best advice I have is if you're experiencing any of the other three types of trigger effects, consider closely what your next words are. Unless those words are along the lines of, "I'm having a little problem processing how I feel about that. Can I take a moment to understand how I feel about that?" you're probably going to say something you regret.

## Why and How Triggers Derail Courageous Conversations

Growing up, I saw tons of TV and print spots warning homeowners about radon gas. The naturally occurring radioactive gas is created from the decomposition of soil, rocks, and ground water. Radon is colorless, odorless, and if inhaled over long periods of time, can cause cancer. You could breathe radon for years and never know of its existence. All that time, the poison creeps through your system, damaging you more with every breath you take.

Triggers in conversations are much like radon. In some circumstances, neither party in a courageous conversation are aware of their, or their conversation partner's, triggers. The original conversation topic comes to a screeching halt when one member of a courageous conversation is triggered. Unless one, or both, conversation partners recognize what's going on, the rest of the conversation is poisoned by the trigger.

What makes being triggered in a courageous conversation so damaging isn't necessarily reliving past traumas, but who you're having the conversation with—the people in our lives that mean the most to us. I know as an academician, I should have charts and research to back this assertion up, but I don't. I can tell you through years of experience in the communication field, I believe that courageous conversations happen in line with the 80–20 Rule.

If you have a business background, you're probably familiar with the 80–20 Rule. If you're new to the concept, here's what it's all about. In the late nineteenth century, Italian economist Vilfredo Federico Damaso Pareto noticed something peculiar with the pea plants in his garden. Pareto observed that 80 percent of the healthy pea pods in his garden came from only 20 percent of the pea plants. Thinking this distribution was odd, Pareto started looking for the 80–20 distribution elsewhere. Astonishingly, the 80–20 ratio was everywhere. Eighty percent of the wealth in Italy, at the time, was held by 20 percent of the population. Across multiple industries, Pareto found that 80 percent of the production came from 20 percent of Italy's companies. The 80–20 ratio was so pervasive that Pareto penned a paper on the phenomena stating that roughly 80 percent of consequences come from 20 percent of causes.[37]

The 80–20 Rule sounds a bit mystical and far afield from courageous conversations and triggers, but I assure you it's not.[38] I would argue that 80 percent of the courageous conversations you are part of happen with the top 20 percent of people who matter the most to you. Spouses, partners, children, parents, close friends, bosses, or anyone else you have a life-changing relationship with make up that top 20 percent. Think about how often you've had a courageous conversation with your barista or the person sitting next to you at a movie as compared to your life partner or your BFF. I'd wager that if you categorized who you're having courageous conversations with, you'd start seeing the 80–20 Rule in full bloom.

What does the 80–20 Rule have to do with triggers? Context. If you're having a courageous conversation with someone close to you and that person triggers you, there's an emotional baggage multiplier. Not only are you dealing with whatever discomfort the trigger caused, but you're also hurt even worse because how could someone close to you not know whatever they did or said was a trigger? This thought often isn't rational. Your conversation partner might not have a clue that their words or actions were a trigger or that you have some undisclosed past trauma. I think of this as when someone wrongs you in a dream and you wake up angry at that person. The person in your dream isn't responsible for what you dreamed, but it hurts nonetheless.

It's at a similar point of irrationality where courageous conversations get derailed. The trigger becomes a double-edged sword. You're dealing with the hurt of past trauma and a perceived defect in a relationship with someone you're close to. That's a lot of outside emotion to bring to any conversation, let alone a conversation you didn't want to have in the first place.

Fortunately, the fact that most of your courageous conversations happen with people who are connected to you closely can be a solution. What would be the worst outcome if you told your partner, close friend, or boss that specific topics triggered you? Do you think that person would run away screaming because of your admission that you have difficulty emotionally processing certain topics? I would wager that most people are more supportive than you give them credit for. If you open up about some of your triggers, your conversation partner will likely share some of their triggers with you. Imagine if 80 percent of your courageous conversations were easier simply because you shared your feelings. Try opening up a few times and see what it does for you. I'm sure the results will be better than you think.

Remember the example of Paul being triggered by his mother's use of the word "choice." After Paul was more self-aware about what was triggering him and derailing his conversations with his mother, he eventually had a courageous conversation with her to share his experiences. He was nervous, but confident that he needed to have the conversation. His *why* was his relationship with his mother. It meant the world to him, and he no longer wanted it to be strained or distant. He called his mother and shared his perspective with her. To his surprise, she was completely unaware of what she was doing and its impact on him. She apologized. She was also honest with him and shared that there is a lack of understanding and sometimes discomfort around the topic because of taboos regarding homosexuality when she grew up. But she assured Paul that she loved him and wanted to be a part of every aspect of his life. Since then, they have had more open and honest conversations.

## Strategies to Deal with Your Triggers

We have discussed the proactive approach to acknowledging and speaking openly about the triggers you are aware of. But that is only half of the equation. There will be instances where triggers you haven't discovered yet will surface in a courageous conversation. Remember, you cannot regulate what you are not aware of. You will more than likely not be able to be mindful of all of your triggers. Some you know, and some you will identify along the way. Look at your self-awareness as a continual and lifelong process. Once you are aware of your triggers, you will be better able to manage them and regulate your emotions. Below is a recap of the solutions we've presented in the chapter around managing your triggers proactively and a few new ideas that will help you from blowing up a courageous conversation from in-the-moment triggers:

- **Feel it.** The first way to identify a trigger is to acknowledge it. Pay attention to your physical response. If you feel that you are being triggered, pause, breathe, and move your mind to curiosity. Then, ask yourself these three questions:
  - What's happening? What was said? What was done?
  - What am I feeling?
  - Why am I feeling this way?

    Be kind to yourself. You may not be able to answer all of these questions at the moment. Often it takes deep self-reflection and vulnerability with yourself.

- **Name it.** Being able to identify what triggers you and then identifying what trauma or past negative experience it pairs with gives you a certain amount of power over that trigger. If you proactively know what your triggers are, you can be on the lookout for them.

- **Find the source.** Remember that there are no triggers without a past trauma or negative experience. If you can identify and heal some from that past trauma, the effects of the trigger should be lessened. Don't be afraid to look to mental health professionals if you need some help addressing past trauma. In the "Exercises and Examples" section of this chapter, I've included a tool that will help you name and find the source of your triggers.

- **Get comfortable with acceptance.** Triggers are 99.99 percent inevitable in your life. I'm sure there's an outlier who has lived a trauma-free life and will never be triggered by anything, but the percentages aren't favorable that you're the unicorn that will never be triggered. Accepting that random people in random conversations will trigger you without knowing they're triggering you is being kind to yourself. Being triggered feels like it's a personal assault, but 99.99 percent of the time that you're triggered by someone, that person has no idea they've caused you harm. Give yourself and the person who has triggered you the grace of knowing the trigger was unintentional.

- **Don't project your triggers.** Much of the time, we become triggered because we're actively shielding ourselves from our past trauma and negative experiences. For example, if you previously had a judgmental and demeaning partner, your mind links the two behaviors. Any time someone disapproves of you, your mind projects that belittling will follow. That's probably not going to happen. Your projection of that additional trigger could further bar you from having a fruitful conversation.

No matter how you're being triggered, my best advice is to hit the pause button in a conversation. I've mentioned this a few times during the chapter because giving yourself the time and space to collect your thoughts before you react to a trigger can mean the difference between a fruitful or a destructive courageous conversation. Take a deep breath, and remember that, more than likely, the person sitting across from you didn't trigger you as part of some evil genius master plan to win the conversation and figure out how to minimize the effects of being triggered. Remember, it's a process. You've got this!

## Recognize If You're Triggering Someone Else

Now that you've got your footing on triggers, it's time to throw a wrench in the works. You're not the only person in a courageous conversation who can or will be triggered. You have just as much chance to say or do something during a courageous conversation that will trigger your conversation partner as you have of being triggered. What's worse than that gaping unknown is that your conversation partner might not understand triggers like you do. That means every courageous conversation is a potential minefield of triggers waiting to be tripped.

Of course, if you go into a courageous conversation knowing what might trigger your conversation partner, stay away from that behavior or topic. In an earlier section, we discussed being triggered by someone looking at their cell phone during a courageous conversation. If you know that behavior sets your conversation partner on edge, turn off your phone before entering the conversation.

If you don't have the luxury of knowing someone's triggers, I hate to drop the bad news, but you'll likely step on a few of those landmines. The trick isn't necessarily avoiding someone else's triggers but knowing how to react if you trigger someone. You will likely not know if you've triggered someone during a conversation, but there may be signs that you're making your conversation partner uncomfortable. When people are triggered, we know it creates a high emotional response often facilitated by a negative response or behavior.

If you see that your conversation partner is getting tense, defensive, or combative, it might be a good time to pause. The key is to be curious and *not* be reactive. Avoid responding negatively to your conversation partner's response to being triggered. Identify that their mood/energy shifted, step back, and be curious. You can ask several questions, such as, "Did I say something or do something that bothered you?" You can also ask, "Is there something about what we're discussing that is making you uncomfortable? If so, we don't have to talk about that now." I pause and ask my conversation partner, "What are you feeling right now?" All of these questions allow for space for your conversation partner to reflect and for you to gain insight. Here are some common signs that show unease in your conversation partner.

- **Shifts**. If your conversation partner suddenly changes the topic, or their breathing rate, field of vision, or the manner in which they're speaking becomes different, those might be signals that they feel uncomfortable. An abrupt change in the way someone is speaking and visual field might be the easiest to spot. If their speech changes rate, volume, or pitch on a dime, it's a sign they're struggling with the conversation. If your conversation partner was looking you in the eye at the beginning of the conversation but they're now avoiding your eyeline, they're probably uncomfortable with the conversation.

- **Nervous energy.** When you become anxious, afraid, or angry, your body reacts by directing energy to your extremities. Someone who is bouncing their leg up and down, drumming their fingers, or rapidly looking from side-to-side might subconsciously be preparing for fight or flight. If you see these signs, check in with your conversation partner and see if a change in topic is in order.

- **Evasive phrases.** If your conversation partner was making direct statements to you at one point in your conversation and is now trying not to make definite statements, you may have wandered into trigger territory. Sudden apologies, hesitation, and vague statements are all indications the conversation is in trouble.[39]

Once again, the best solution, if your conversation partner is showing any of these signs, is to stop the conversation and check in with them. Unless a conversation is literally a life-or-death matter, I cannot think of any courageous conversations that are worth needlessly damaging a relationship by ignoring triggers. The upside to being curious about your conversation partner's triggers and comfort level is that you have the opportunity to open a dialogue about triggers. If you and your conversation partner can have a frank and open discussion about topics and behaviors that are triggering, you'll have made a huge stride in your relationship. You'll be aware of each other's triggers, and hopefully, future courageous conversations will go more smoothly.

## Pitfalls to Avoid

There are a few pitfalls you should be aware of when discussing similar triggers with your conversation partner. The first is being dismissive of your conversation partner's triggers because your reaction to a similar trauma isn't as severe as theirs is. Imagine that you and your conversation partner were riding together in the back seat of a car. A truck swerves into your lane and hits the vehicle you're traveling in head-on. You and your conversation partner get out of the car with different injuries. You came through with a few bruises and cuts while your conversation partner's legs were broken. Even though you were sitting next to each other in the same car and experienced the same accident, your traumas were vastly different.

In the car crash example, a reasonable person would not expect their conversation partner to be up to go out dancing a week after the accident. However, it's common for people with similar traumas not to understand the severity, or lack thereof, of the other's pain. "I got over that and moved on. Why can't you?" is usually the mentality of comparative traumas. When you take this attitude towards your conversation partner's triggers, you're making an uninformed judgment. The best tactic here is to respectfully listen to your conversation partner's story and make no value judgments on how that trauma affects them.

The second pitfall is exactly the opposite of dismissing your conversation partner's experiences. I've heard this called the Great Pain Off or the Trauma Olympics. This is where you try to match or exceed your conversation partner's trigger story. Think of sitting around at a family function, and your great-aunts start telling each other about their medical problems. One aunt complains that her cataract surgery was so painful she couldn't sleep for a week. The other aunt chimes in that she swears getting a new hip meant she couldn't sleep for a month. The Great Pain Off with the aunts continues with increasingly gruesome stories of medical issues until a fed-up cousin tactfully changes the subject.

There's nothing wrong with sharing traumatic experiences with your conversation partner, if it's done correctly. In many cases being vulnerable enough to explain why you react a certain way can help both members of a courageous conversation understand each other. That happens when the intent of telling your trigger story is for a win-win outcome. If you're trying to one-up or dismiss your conversation partner's trigger story, you've slipped into the win-lose category. You are trying to win the conversation by mitigating your conversation partner's triggers and that's not cool. You'll end up alienating your conversation partner and achieving nothing.

Finally, there's the fixer. This is when your conversation partner discloses their trigger story, and you try to repair their trauma. Usually, the fixer response to a trigger story is well-intentioned enough. Most people have a natural inclination to help or give advice. However, chances are that you are throwing out some platitudes, folk wisdom, or Insta-tok posts that aren't going to magically change someone's trauma. I'd also stay away from telling your conversation partner the story of how someone you know resolved similar issues. Usually, the best thing you can do is to ask how and if you can be helpful. If the answer is "you can't," accept that. If your conversation partner needs something from you, be sure you follow through with it. Aside from being the right thing to do, taking the action your conversation partner requested builds trust, and trust makes any courageous conversation easier.

## The Wrap-Up

The discussion of triggers is more of an introspective step in the ACTER model than an action step. You can make statements to your conversation partner to show them that you're curious about what they have to say. Triggers are more about being aware of yourself and using that knowledge as a signpost for conversational pitfalls. With this heightened sense of awareness, if you are triggered in a courageous conversation, you have more of a fighting chance to not let it tank the rest of your discussion. The next area in the ACTER model, emotional regulation, will give you the skills to ensure that you can keep your reaction to those triggers in check.

For now, catalog and trace back as many triggers as you can. The process isn't always pleasant, and you might need some outside help along the way. Nothing good comes from burying or ignoring topics, phrases, events, or circumstances that produce uncomfortable emotional responses. In the "Exercises and Examples" section below, there's a tool that will help you chart out your triggers and examine them. Only do what you feel comfortable with. When delving into triggers, I've found that the first few are incredibly difficult to sort out, but the process gets easier the more you do it. Take your time and be kind to yourself during the process. I assure you, you're doing better at all of this than you think!

# Chapter 4—Exercises and Examples: Triggers

**Exercise: The Trigger Worksheet**

Much like the Curiosity Worksheet in the previous chapter, this framework is best used before you enter a courageous conversation. The table below is designed to help you track and analyze your triggers. If you see that you're being triggered in a courageous conversation and understand where your emotion responses are coming from, you can formulate a plan to regulate that emotion response more easily.

The chart below gives you an example trigger and different characteristics you can use to help identify a trigger's effect on you. I've listed five common example triggers to show you how the exercise works. Below is a breakdown of the topics and what they mean. After you've read the example triggers, feel free to make a chart of your own and list your trigger, responses, behavior tendencies, and drivers of behavior.

**Trigger:** Topics, phrases, events, or circumstances that produce an uncomfortable emotional response.

**Response:** How you feel immediately after you've been triggered. Remember, there can, and likely will, be more than one type of response associated with a trigger. Earlier in this chapter we explored mental, physical, emotional, and verbal responses to triggers. On your list, write down any specific responses that fall into any of these categories.

**Behavior Tendency:** This is how you are likely to react to your conversation partner after being triggered. These tendencies will not necessarily be rational. The first example trigger is being interrupted or talked over. The behavioral tendency for this example is to shut down or get quiet. You might think that the behavior tendency should be to shout or get louder than your conversation partner to be heard. In this case, the person who is being triggered gets quiet because they feel that nothing they have to say will matter to their conversation partner, so why bother shouting to get the point across? There's nothing right or wrong about that tendency. Whatever your behavior tendency is, it will be unique to you.

**Driver of Behavior**: This category is the meat and potatoes of this exercise. The driver of the behavior examines why you react to a trigger in the way you do. Going back to the first trigger, the driver of this behavior is: I feel the need to feel heard or understood. You can go as far down the rabbit hole on the driver of the behavior as you wish. The driver of this behavior could also have been: I felt the need to feel heard or understood because I was a middle child and felt that my parents and siblings never noticed my accomplishments. Be as honest and open with yourself as you feel comfortable with. Remember that the greater your level of introspection, the more quickly you'll be able to develop strategies to regulate your emotional response.

After you've read through the examples in the table below, feel free to create your own trigger worksheet to track and analyze your specific triggers. I have set up a password-protected Excel spreadsheet to track my triggers. That way, I can freely record my thoughts without fear of anyone accidentally stumbling on this highly personal information. I try to record the trigger, emotional response, and behavioral tendency as soon after the trigger event as possible. The farther away from an event you get, the greater the chance your mind might soften your responses to your trigger.

Don't feel that you must understand the driver of your behavior immediately. If this is the first time you've thought about triggers and how you react to them, you won't understand your behavior right away, and that's okay. It might take you days or even weeks to understand the roots of your behavior. So go back and review your list of triggers periodically and spend some quiet time reflecting on why you react the way you do.

| Trigger | Response | Behavior Tendency | Driver of Behavior |
|---|---|---|---|
| Being interrupted or talked over. | Disrespected. | Shut down or get quiet. | No voice as a child. No I have a need to feel heard or understood. |
| Being invalidated. | Resentful. | Get defensive / yell in an effort to convince, or shut down and stop sharing with them. | I feel unheard and that my experiences / feelings are not valid. |
| Criticism. | Feeling judged. | Deflect. Bring up things from the past and remind them of all their mistakes. | Strong need for perfectionism. |
| A forceful demand from another person. | Helplessness or loss of control. | Combative and reject demand, or passive aggressive and agree with no intention of complying. | Past experiences with loss of agency and control. |

*Examples*

**Why Am I Always the Bad Guy?**

Kim and Donita have two lovely children, ages four and seven. Both children are at that age where their curiosity about the world around them intersects with pushing boundaries. Neither child is anywhere near what you might consider "bad kids," but from time to time their parents need to reinforce the consequences of unacceptable behavior. The brunt of discipline has always fallen to Donita. It took a few years for Donita to catch on that her husband was actively avoiding disciplining their children. The boilermaker moment for Donita was during a church event. The kids were running around in the fellowship hall and almost knocked over an elderly woman using a walker. Kim was watching the kids, saw what happened, and apologized to the little old lady. However, Kim said nothing to the children about their behavior.

Kim's reluctance to discipline their children comes from some unsavory punishment tactics employed on him by his parents. When he was growing up in the 1980s, Kim's parents believed in "spare the rod and spoil the child." There were nights Kim went to bed with a bruised backside and no dinner to show him the error of his ways. Kim's parents always reminded him that they wished Kim hadn't forced them to do this, but that his behavior forced them to use such tactics. Anytime the topic of disciplining his own children came up, Kim became triggered and avoided the topic at all costs.

When Kim and Donita returned home from church, they put the kids to bed and had a chat.

"What happened tonight? I don't understand why you didn't tell the kids to stop running around Mrs. Shaw. I saw you looking at them, and you just stood there. Kim, I can't always be the bad guy when it comes to the kids. It's not fair to me and doesn't send a good message to them," said Donita.

Kim couldn't look Donita in the eye and began to bounce his leg up and down. After a moment of silence, Kim replied, "Well, you see ... I really didn't ... It happened pretty quickly. I just ..."

Even though Kim was evasive during any conversation that dealt with discipline, Donita thought something about Kim's reaction tonight was unusual. Rather than disengaging, as she often did when Kim mealymouthed around accounting for himself, Donita thought she would try a different tactic.

"Kim, this seems to have upset you more than usual. Is there something that happened tonight that I don't know about?"

"No. There's nothing that happened *tonight* that you don't know about," said Kim, looking his wife straight in the eye.

There was something in the way Kim said "tonight" that didn't feel right to Donita and she continued, "Kim, what am I missing? Every time we talk about correcting the kids, you check out. I've seen you talk to your employees at work, and you're not shy about giving feedback. Help me understand what's happening here."

"I'll try. But I promise you that there are reasons I get freaked out when it comes to disciplining our kids," said Kim.

"That's progress. I'm on your side, and I want us to figure this out at your pace. Do you feel like talking a little more tonight?" asked Donita.

"Maybe. It has to do with when I was a kid," said Kim.

## Rotten Feedback

"Don't worry about shutting the door behind you."

Marcus entered his boss Belinda's office and left the door open as requested. Belinda's office was positioned right outside her department's cube farm and keeping her door open while speaking to a department head generally wasn't a horrible thing. Belinda's morning routine was to ask team leads, like Marcus, into her office and check in for the day's tasks. Everyone in the department had the benefit of hearing the day's tasks. At other times, like this morning, Belinda's open-door talks weren't helpful at all.

Belinda motioned for Marcus to sit down and the pair exchanged pleasantries before Belinda cut to the chase.

"How do you think your team did on the Finch project?"

*The Finch project ... the Finch project ...* thought Marcus. There wasn't anything currently on the books for Finch Electronics. The last thing his department did was—"Are you talking about that rush price sheet and scope of work we did for Finch three weeks ago right before the Fourth of July?" asked Marcus.

"Yes, that's what I'm talking about," said Belinda, more tersely than was necessary.

Marcus was a little taken off guard but replied to the best of his recollection. "Uhhh ... we dropped what we were doing before the shutdown on the Fourth and got you the information you requested."

"Well, there were a number of typos and Finch said the pricing was off. Why didn't you follow up with them on this?"

Marcus's face felt flush, and he started sweating. All of this happened long enough ago and was a minor request, so Marcus was having trouble remembering all of the specifics. As far as he knew, the price sheet and scope of work were just a thumbnail for the sales team. Marcus didn't think that the materials his team had rushed out before the holiday were for the folks at Finch.

*And everyone in the department can hear her dressing me down and I sound like I don't know what I'm talking about. I don't know what I'm talking about because I don't have my project notes*, thought Marcus as he was nearing a meltdown point.

Marcus took a second before totally spiraling out of control. He knew that his boss's actions were triggering some deep-rooted insecurities and he needed to get a handle on the situation. He took a deep breath and focused on the problem at hand. How could he pause the conversation and what did he need to sort this out with his boss?

*My notes!*

"Ma'am, this was a couple weeks back, so would you mind if I grabbed my notes on Finch? With those, I'm sure I can help sort out whatever has gone wrong with the process."

Belinda nodded and Marcus scurried to his cube to get his notes. When he returned, he didn't bother asking and shut the door before trying to figure out what kind of goat rodeo he'd walked into.

_____

_____

_____

_____

_____

_____

| Trigger | Response | Behavior Tendency | Driver of Behavior |
|---------|----------|-------------------|--------------------|
|         |          |                   |                    |
|         |          |                   |                    |
|         |          |                   |                    |
|         |          |                   |                    |

## CHAPTER 5

# E—Emotional Regulation

Now that we have a handle on triggers and better understand what pushes our buttons, it's time to develop strategies to keep our emotions on an even keel during courageous conversations. The principles of EI govern all the strategies we'll discuss in this chapter. We considered the basics of EI in this book's introduction, but revisiting the concept will help frame your mindset for this step of the ACTER model.

Throughout the steps of the ACTER model, you've been exposed to elements of EI. Appreciating a diversity of opinions and curiosity gives us the ability to effectively acknowledge the emotions of ourselves and others. The techniques that were discussed in the "Triggers" chapter and will be discussed in the "Respectful Listening" chapter help us identify our emotion's origins. Communicating our emotions effectively is in the realm of emotional regulation.

The difference between EI and emotional regulation might sound like a matter of semantics, but I assure you it's not. The distinction between the two concepts is like the gap between intelligence and wisdom. I define intelligence as the accumulation of raw knowledge and wisdom as the ability to apply your intelligence deftly. A typical description of the distinction is that someone has book sense (intelligence) but no common sense (wisdom). In this chapter, I'll call on you to apply your EI to recognize when to emotionally regulate. Remember, EI is the ability to effectively acknowledge, identify, regulate, and communicate your emotions, as well as understanding the emotions of others. Emotional regulation is the ability to understand the source and extent of your emotions and how the expressions of your emotions affect a courageous conversation.

In this chapter, you'll learn that emotional regulation has internal and external components. When you avoid letting your emotions get the best of you, that's internal emotional regulation. The external element of emotional regulation has to do with how your actions can cause an adverse emotional reaction in your conversation partner. We've all been guilty of needling someone during a conversation, and you'll learn some common pitfalls when you want to covertly lash out because your emotions are screaming for scorched earth.

Before you jump into these techniques, I want to clarify that emotional regulation doesn't mean that having an emotional reaction is bad or that the feelings you have during a courageous conversation are invalid. Emotion is why we have most of our courageous conversations in the first place. Generally, one party in a courageous conversation has a passionate belief or value which the other party might not share. I'm not suggesting that you dull your sparkle regarding the things you hold dear. I am saying that you should regulate your emotions to the point that you can have a productive and civil conversation with someone else. Feeling anger during a courageous conversation is fine. Flipping over a table because you're angry at your conversation partner's stance isn't.

## Strong Emotions

Although it's the most accessible emotion associated with a courageous conversation, anger isn't the only emotion that can bubble up when talking to someone. The topic of conversation and your triggers can elicit a rainbow of emotions. Remember in the "Curiosity" chapter, we discussed the social issues collage. We all walk into courageous conversations with strong emotions. Be mindful of where you stand emotionally around a topic. Also, remember that your triggers aren't the only thing that will cause you to have an emotional response. Your conversation partner could tell a sad story about their past or inform you of an unconscionable situation.

Because of the context and range that covers emotional regulation, you'll see the term "strong emotions" used often in this chapter. You may have thought that regulating your emotions in a courageous conversation only applies to anger or other feelings that are considered negative. But, emotions that are generally held to be being positive can be harmful to a courageous conversation as well. Consider saying, "I love you" to someone. On its face, what could possibly be wrong with expressing fondness for someone else? The difficulty of the phrase is context. Saying you love your mother is one thing, but expressing strong affection for someone after an amazing first date may be problematic.

You should avoid making statements that express excessively positive or negative emotions during a courageous conversation. When demonstrating strong emotions, you risk the conversation shifting from the topic at hand to the connotations of the emotions being expressed. For example, while discussing if NSYNC or Backstreet Boys were the best boy band, you start waving your arms around and raising the volume of your voice.

Your conversation partner might shift the discussion from Justin Timberlake's merits to why you're suddenly acting mad.

Strong emotions can also arise when you have a historical connection or proximity to the topic you're discussing. If your favorite boy band in high school was NSYNC, debating whether the Backstreet Boys were a better band might become heated because of your nostalgic connection. Our historical context impacts how we see the world and how we emotionally respond. Our experiences influence what we define as good or bad, right or wrong, and where our passions and fears lie. That is why it is important to understand as much about yourself as possible when you go into a courageous conversation. The questions I encourage you to be curious about are, "How do I feel about this topic/issue?" and "What life experiences have I had associated with this topic/subject?"

My experiences have impacted my perspective on specific topics. I had the privilege of growing up with two uncles in the LGBTQIA+ community. As a young child, I fondly remember coming home after school to my uncles' friends and listening to them talk and laugh. I also watched them suffer grief and sorrow as their friends became ill and died from AIDS. I listened to them share their struggles about coming out to family, fear of violence, and being gay or trans in the 1980s black community. Seeing my uncles' experiences is part of my historical context. As a result of these intimate experiences, I have a deep understanding of and proximity to the LGBTQIA+ community that I must understand that many people do not. This personal experience with the LGBTQIA+ community makes me more sensitive and passionate about issues around this topic, and my perspective is likely different from that of others.

As with all of the elements of the ACTER Model, the key to managing strong emotions is curiosity and self-awareness. The more you understand why you feel the way you do, the easier it will be to create strategies to regulate strong emotions when those topics arise. Knowledge of the past isn't the only factor you'll contend with in regulating your emotions. You'll have to combat your unique biology.

## Emotions, Logic, and Brain Processing

Before we can learn about how to regulate our emotions, it's helpful to understand how and why humans have emotions in the first place. The science of emotions is an incredibly complex topic that runs far afield from this text. I'll present the high points to give you context for why you feel the way that you do.

On a physiological level, the process that creates emotions inside us is biological forces, as we discussed in the "Triggers" chapter. External stimuli are cataloged and processed by our brains. Different parts of our brains react to those stimuli by creating various chemicals called neurotransmitters. There are over fifty known types of neurotransmitters, and they all have different functions within our brains. Some neurotransmitters control bodily functions like blood pressure and breathing. Other neurotransmitters, like serotonin or dopamine, help to manage our moods.

Unless you're taking medication that regulates or modifies the output of neurotransmitters, you're stuck with which and what level of neurotransmitters your brain decides to pump out. So, there's not much you or I can do about the biochemistry functionality of our emotional state. Think about the last time you were startled. Your brain reacts to that fright by producing epinephrine, which triggers a fight, flight, or freeze impulse throughout your brain. Those chemical reactions are the reality of our feelings and fall within three different categories:

- **Physiological response**: These are responses to stimuli that create physical changes in our body. For example, feeling afraid may lead to an increased heart rate, rapid breathing, and sweating. Some of these responses were discussed in the "Triggers" chapter.

- **Subjective experience**: This component refers to the conscious awareness of emotion and how it feels to the individual experiencing it. It includes the person's interpretation of the emotion—positive or negative, intense or mild, and so on. If you receive the stimulus of a birthday present, you might describe your subjective experience as feeling joyous, content, or elated.

- **Behavioral or expressive response**: Emotions can be expressed through various behaviors, such as facial expressions, body language, and verbal communication. Someone who is happy may smile, laugh, and show enthusiasm. A person who is angry may frown, clench their fists or raise their voice. Behavioral responses can be deliberate or automatic, and they can also vary depending on cultural norms and social context.

There is little you can do to regulate or override physiological responses. If you're having a conversation in your office break room and a light fixture falls out of the ceiling, at that moment, you and your conversation partner will both exhibit signs of being startled, and your heart and breathing rate will probably rise rapidly. Given the unexpected nature of the event, you probably won't be able to regulate your behavioral response either. An automatic vocal response might be to yell, "Watch out!" if you notice the light fixture falling, or you may even jump away from the falling object. All of this is your brain managing your response. Even if you tried, it would be hard to regulate or override the natural reactions laid out above. What you can control in this situation is your subjective response. Do you become enraged by the incident and look for who to blame because you almost got killed? Do you fuss at your conversation partner putting you in harm's way because they suggested meeting in the break room? That's certainly one way to go, but it's an irrational emotional response. Unless your conversation partner sets up an elaborate trap in the breakroom, your outburst will damage your relationship and reputation. This shows us the power of our brains and how we feel and respond.

As goofy as it sounds, we've all had ridiculous emotional outbursts like the light fixture example. It may be a bit confusing that I said that there is little you can do to regulate or override physiological responses. While there are things that you can do things to enhance or minimize your physiological responses, you cannot stop your body from responding to stimuli and processing and feeling fear, sadness, or joy. However, you *can* regulate and control your subjective responses. In the light fixture example, regulating your response would mean not voicing your conspiracy theories.

To understand emotional regulation, we first must examine the impact of emotions on brain processing. Years ago, I came across a book by Larry Senn called *The Mood Elevator: Take Charge of Your Feelings, Become a Better You.* Senn provided two practical charts illustrating the impact of our emotions on our brain processing. The first chart shows different aspects of brain function in a calm state. The first step is memory and proceeds into higher functionality.

## CALM EMOTIONAL STATE
### Full Access to All Functions of Our Brain

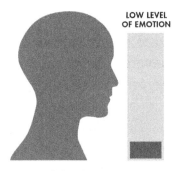

**LOW LEVEL OF EMOTION**

**LOW EMOTION**
(calm, relaxed)

- wisdom
- insight / judgement
- common sense
- empathy
- emotional regulation
- information processing
- perception
- analysis
- critical thinking
- memory

What Senn explains in this chart is that when we are in a calm emotional state, we have access to all functions of our brain. This includes wisdom, insight, judgment, common sense, empathy, emotional regulation, information processing, perception, analysis, critical thinking, and memory. However, in the second illustration provided by Senn, reproduced below, he shows the loss of functionality of the brain as a result of high/negative emotions. Essentially, he contends that when we experience high emotions, we lose access to the higher levels of our brain functionality.

## HIGH EMOTIONAL STATE
### Blocks Access to Higher Levels

**HIGH LEVEL OF EMOTION**

- wisdom
- insight / judgement
- common sense
- empathy
- emotional regulation

- information processing
- perception
- analysis
- critical thinking
- memory

**HIGH EMOTION**
(anger, fear, excitement, love, disgust, frustration)

I had a mentor early in my career tell me, "High emotions cancel out logical thinking." That has stuck with me for years, and it speaks to the impact of emotions on our rational brain. There has been extensive research on how emotions affect logic and reasoning. According to Shona Adams, author of the paper "Are Cognitive Distortions Much More Important Than You Realized?," high emotional arousal inhibits brain regions necessary for logical and complex reasoning.[40] Here's what emotions and thinking look like in the real world. If you see a ferocious lion in front of you, you may be perfectly calm if the lion is behind bars in a zoo. However, if there is any element of doubt about your safety, like the back gate being open, the emotional part of your brain will take over and classify the situation in terms of fear. This emotion of fear is what signals your body to be ready to run and protect yourself from potential danger.

Look at the second chart provided by Larry Senn. When fear is high in a panic, your senses become heightened, and you are aware of the danger in front of you (perception). Your eyes may dart around quickly to analyze the situation (analysis). Your brain is running a mile a minute processing what it is seeing or experiencing (information processing). You use everything you can think of to figure a way out as quickly as possible (critical thinking and memory). Even with this breakdown, I am sure you are still curious as to why the emotional side of our brains completely takes over our logical minds. While complex, it is pretty simple. Our logical brain is responsible for our deep and rational thinking. While deep and rational thinking are usually important, in a moment of impending danger, they are not. Your logical brain will be too busy calculating potential risks to consider the long-term implications of your actions. How often have you heard someone who was part of a scary situation say, "I didn't even think. I just ran."? The fear from their emotional brain is what drove that, not the logic. So, if there is a potential threat and things aren't entirely safe, the emotional part of our brain will take over to help us respond quickly to danger, which may save our lives. While this is wonderful and life-saving if a ferocious lion is in front of us, when emotionally triggered in a courageous conversation, the result is impaired judgment and words we may regret.

Let's review how this works based on everything we've learned in this section, using the light fixture falling as our stimulus. When the light fixture begins to fall, your brain starts pumping out neurotransmitters. Some neurotransmitter triggers reach back into our brain's data banks and pull out a memory of what happens when objects fall. Your brain processes those memories and picks the most applicable ones to analyze. Your mental computer says that falling objects aren't good for you, and your perception now is to get as far away from the falling object as possible.

The physical threat is over once the light fixture hits the floor, but the emotional experience is not. Your brain still has all those emotion-inducing chemicals floating around. You now have a choice. Either you get stuck on the perspective floor or ride the elevator up to the common-sense phase. In the lower levels, we tend to lose access to our common sense and wisdom. This is why smart people sometimes do things that aren't so smart, and your perspective gets skewed. Being upset by what is clearly a freak accident or making irrational statements about your conversation partner trying to kill you is low-level emotional brain processing. If you pause, take a breath, and allow your rational brain back on board the train, your perspective transcends into common sense, insight, and wisdom. This looks like checking to see if you were injured, determining you're okay, and then asking your conversation partner if they're hurt.

That explanation may seem drawn out, but emotions can be difficult to understand in the best of circumstances. The more you can break down what's happening inside your head, the greater your ability to identify what and where your emotions are coming from. That's the basis for EI and the first step to regulating our emotions.

Even though I've taken a step-by-step clinical approach to understanding the source of our emotions and identifying how to regulate them, this process isn't a foolproof formula. It's more like baking a cake. If you've never tried to bake a cake, you can follow the instructions to a tee, and still, outside factors can ruin your hard work and efforts. Humidity, old baking powder, or an uncalibrated oven can make your cake inedible even though you followed the recipe.

If you really want cake and it doesn't turn out right, you adjust and try to bake another cake. You learn not to bake on humid days, adjust baking times for your rickety old stove, and go to the store to buy new baking powder. You, of course, can see where this is going. EI is not about perfection. It's about progress. You're not going to achieve the heights of EI every time you try. But if you don't keep trying and adjusting for your personal variables, you're never going to get there.

Remember, you cannot regulate what you are not aware of. Logically, the first step to emotional regulation is acknowledging that you have emotions. That means permitting yourself to feel. To do this, be intentional about tapping into your emotions as you experience them. Each moment gives you a data point to understand yourself better. Every time you have an emotional experience, try to take a step back and catalog what emotion you are feeling. Ask yourself: "What am I feeling?" and "Why am I feeling it?" That emotional experience doesn't have to be during a courageous conversation. Start mentally cataloging your emotions in multiple settings. From walking out and seeing that you've got a flat tire to hearing you're a new aunt, identifying and cataloging any emotional experience creates more self-awareness and understanding of your emotions. Creating a heightened sense of awareness when the stakes are low is beneficial because I can assure you that trying to build this level of awareness is much more difficult when you're in the heat of the moment. We often forget that there's a higher purpose afoot when a grocery bag breaks while you're trying to unlock your front door.

When I first tried to understand how and where my emotions were coming from, I wasn't concerned with analyzing what I felt while it was happening. I thought I was doing well if I could look back five or ten minutes after an emotional event and analyze my emotional response. However, if I responded inappropriately, the damage was already done. My goal was to evaluate my emotional state closer to the event. My competitive nature turned that goal into a game. I constantly tried to break my personal best time. When I started tracking my emotions and my emotional responses as the emotional event happened, I could start to see patterns, tendencies, and behaviors. I could see my emotions were different during different times of the day. Once I was able to proactively mitigate a negative tendency that I had in real time, I knew I was growing. The funny thing is, in this game, I doubt I will ever "win." It's about small victories because every situation in life brings about different emotions and responses. I'd strongly suggest putting some framework in place to categorize your emotional experiences and responses. You'll never be able to regulate your emotions if you can't see the path your emotions are making through your mind.

## The Power of Choice

You may have noticed that I haven't used the term "control your emotions" in this chapter. That's because controlling your emotions is impossible. The different stimuli produced in your brain are inevitable, whether you like it or not, meaning the mind and body will always respond to stimuli. What we can control is regulating what we do when emotional waves hit. Emotional regulation is the set of skills you'll employ to respond to your emotions.

Emotional regulation is grounded in the premise of stimulus and response. When someone does something or says something to you, and you feel a strong emotion hit you—that is the stimulus. As humans, we tend to respond immediately to the stimulus. When we do that, we give the emotion power. But there is another option. Between stimulus and response is *choice*—choosing how you respond despite the emotion you feel. I can respond based on my current feelings about what you said or did, or I can choose to respond based on who I am, my values, and my character. In important relationships, we can choose to respond based on our role in maintaining the relationship. Emotional regulation in courageous conversations is based on the principle that your reactions are *not* based on what your conversation partner did or said. Still, your responses are rooted in who you are and your values. That means if your conversation partner is being a jerk, you don't have to respond in kind (unless your value set calls for you to be a jerk; in that case, you probably should have put this book down a while back). You have the power of choice. When you let your emotions dictate actions contrary to your values, you're harming yourself.

Remember the story of the coworkers Anne and Jim? After Jim told Anne why minority scholarships are important, she was confronted with a topic that she disagreed with. Based on Anne's response, the emotion that she felt may have been disgust, disagreement, or anger. At that moment, she responded based on her emotion. However, what if Anne had paused between the stimulus and her response to Jim and explored her power of choice instead? She could have asked herself, *What impact will my words have on this relationship?* We all know the adage, "think before you speak." When my clients find themselves triggered, I tell them to feel the emotion, then pause and take a breath. I advise them, before they respond and during that moment of pause, to ask themselves these three questions:

- "What is the goal/purpose of the statement I am about to make?"
- "What may be the impact of the statement that I am about to make?"
- "What is the value in the statement that I am about to make?"

138

These are always powerful questions to reflect on when we are emotionally triggered, as they give us agency over our words, behaviors, and actions.

## Self-Awareness

You can only go so long before emotional reactions create actions contrary to your values. When we push our values aside and allow ourselves to become bound to our emotions, it can make us feel like we're failing as a person, parent, spouse, or boss. You're not failing at anything. You're human. But you must decide to exhibit emotional regulation to avoid internal and external discord. Eventually, poor emotional regulation spills out into your personal relationships and social interactions. If one of your values is treating others as you want to be treated, but you make a buddy feel guilty for not wanting to hang out, your emotional regulations and values are out of whack.

At its core, emotional regulation is about managing our emotions in a way that allows us to navigate all of life's challenges, even courageous conversations. Emotional regulation is learning to accept our emotions without judgment. This means recognizing that all emotions are valid and that it's okay to feel whatever you feel. It's also important to avoid self-criticism or negative self-talk, as this can make it more difficult to manage our emotions. You should aim to be compassionate and understanding with yourself by recognizing that emotions are a natural part of the human experience.

An easy way to give yourself grace when trying to regulate your emotions is to remember that what you're feeling isn't permanent. Think about the most extreme emotions you've ever felt. Those volatile times might have been at your wedding or during a funeral. Whenever you felt a spike in your emotional state, those emotions passed. You may still grieve the loss of a loved one, but the intensity of that feeling isn't the same as it was during the eulogy. During courageous conversations, if you can hold on to the kernel of truth that whatever you're feeling at that moment will change, you will be able to implement a way to regulate your emotions.

## Strategies to Combat Negative Emotional Responses

You and I might not have the same emotional reality because of the chemicals our brains are pumping out. But we do control how we react to the storm of chemicals churning in our noggins. If you can pause just for a few seconds before letting your emotions get the best of you, you can employ one of the following five strategies to regulate how you express your emotions.

### Avoid Hyperbole

Hyperbolic statements are intentional exaggerations that are intended to emphasize a point rather than be taken literally. Some examples of hyperbole are:

"I've told you a thousand times that. . ."
"You can't believe anything from that source."
"I'd rather die than talk about that."

Of course, none of the above statements are factual. It's doubtful that everything someone says is a fib or that death is preferable to speaking about a topic.

Hyperbole is one of those instances where emotional regulation takes aim at your conversation partner. When you use hyperbolic statements in a courageous conversation, you're likely trying to make a dig at your conversation partner rather than emphasizing a point. In doing so, you're attempting to get your conversation partner to lose their cool. Playing the "goading someone else into getting mad" game never ends well. If you feel yourself starting to exaggerate for any reason, try injecting constructive truth and curiosity into your statements. Here's how you can change the previous three hyperbolic statements into something more positive:

"It feels like I've mentioned that before. If I haven't, would you like to discuss it further?"

"Some of the articles I've seen from that newspaper are a little light on sources. Can we look up those claims together and see what's really going on?"

"Discussing that topic makes me uncomfortable. Can we tread lightly as we talk about that?"

Keeping your statements honest and factual leaves your conversation partner no chance to misinterpret your meaning.

## Avoid Assumptions and Storytelling

We all know the saying around assumptions—no need for me to repeat it here. We know that assumptions are harmful in relationships, especially in courageous conversations. I use the term *assumptions*, but I also like to explore the story we tell ourselves as a result of the assumptions we make. Remember Paul and his mother? After Paul's courageous conversation, I encouraged him to be curious about his mother and ask her about her thoughts on being gay. What he found out was astonishing. She shared with him what it was like for people who were gay when she grew up and what she was taught. She explained that during her time, being gay was so taboo that she did not see or know of anyone who was gay. She shared with him that what she remembers most is that people who were gay were ostracized and excluded. She knows that times are different now, but she is still scared for him: scared that someone will harm him or treat him differently.

Paul did not know his mother felt this way. After her use of the word "choice" triggered him, the story Paul told himself was that his mother was intolerant and uninterested in that part of his life. He never even imagined she was concerned for him. The stories we tell ourselves are just as powerful as our lived experiences. They block communication and understanding. Without curiosity, our assumptions and stories will validate our imagination and create a false reality. Before you respond to an assumption, ask yourself, "What is the story that I am telling myself?" In safe courageous conversations, I tell clients to be vulnerable and share the story they were telling themselves with their conversation partner. They are often surprised by the starkly different reality and can remove the imagined barriers assumptions can bring about.

## Be Curious

If you can't think of anything that isn't negative or hurtful to say to your conversation partner, fall back on the phrases of curiosity we discussed in Chapter 3. Remember that the goal of any courageous conversation is to expand our perspective and understand our conversation partner's point of view. Asking questions about your conversation partner's positions or experiences may diffuse your emotional response to their statement. Your strong emotional response may be due to your conversation partner not phrasing their thoughts clearly, or making an offhanded comment that you hear out of context. Give your conversation partner a little grace and fully understand the point they're trying to make before you let your emotions get the best of you.

## Pause and Breathe

When you identify that you may have a strong emotional reaction to a conversation, this technique to diffuse poor responses may be the simplest to remember and easiest to implement: Take a three-second pause before responding to any statement from your conversation partner. Don't estimate three seconds and speak—do a mental count of one-one thousand, two-one thousand, three-one thousand. Redirecting your thoughts by taking a three-second count gives you a short respite to balance your next statement for the good of the conversation.

## Assume Positive Intentions

When we are emotionally triggered, our emotions take over our logical brain, and we tend to tell ourselves stories about the other person and their intentions. When I work with clients, I suggest they pause their brains and assume positive intentions when they are triggered. Assuming positive intentions is when you pause your brain and work from the assumption that the person you are in dialogue with is inherently good, fair, and honest. Please assume that the intent behind their words is not ill-intentioned or malicious. Set aside your judgments and preconceived notions and give the person the benefit of the doubt. When you assume positive intentions, it suspends immediate judgment and allows for curiosity. So, the next time you are triggered, don't automatically assume the other person meant any harm. Assume positive intentions and be curious. What if your conversation partner's statement was based on their limited experience or knowledge? What if their statements were made because their worldview has never been questioned? What if they are insecure right now, and this is their defense mechanism? When you assume positive intentions, it allows you to respond with more questions rather than defensive statements.

## Unhealthy Conversation Strategies

So far, we've discussed emotional regulation as an internal exercise—meaning not losing your temper or saying something hurtful during a conversation. There is also an external component to emotional regulation that is often overlooked. Not only must you rein in your emotions, but you also need to be aware of your conversation partner's emotions. As you know, this book only focuses on the things you can control. Therefore, it is not your responsibility to regulate the emotions of your conversation partner. Where you play a role in the emotions of your conversation partner is how you engage with them. Humans know how to push buttons or use creative strategies to get their way. Sometimes, we say, "The hell with it!" and *choose* to provoke an emotional response from our conversation partner. If your first thought after reading that was, *What? I'd never do something like that …* I'd bet a paycheck that you've tried to play on someone's emotions during a conversation to get your desired outcome.

Conversational manipulation is something humans grow up doing. Have you ever seen a toddler speak overly affectionately toward a parent to get a cookie? How about the old, "Why can't I do that? Mom said I could before she went to work." When toddlers act out or make outrageous statements, it's because they want attention. Many of us haven't left those manipulative tendencies behind in adulthood. If you've ever tried to make your conversation partner get angry so you can "win" a conversation or become syrupy sweet to sway someone's opinion—you're a toddler in an adult's clothing.

I don't believe that most people intend to be manipulative during a courageous conversation. Most simply wish to be heard, understood, and validated. However, when your conversation partner presents differing opinions, the tendency is to turn the conversation into a competition. (Refer to the "Conversational Goals" section in Chapter 1 if you need a refresher on diffusing competition in conversations.) Below are examples of manipulative tactics that may present during a courageous conversation. Be mindful of these behaviors in yourself, but also be on the lookout for them from your conversation partner.

## Guilt-Tripping

Guilt-tripping is when you try to make someone else feel responsible for your actions or decisions. Within the context of courageous conversations, a guilt trip usually takes the form of: "I did this for or because of you, so you should do or feel this way for me." If you reduce a courageous conversation to an emotionally charged transaction, you're missing the point of the conversation. Your number-one goal in a courageous conversation is to be curious about your conversation partner, not to leverage your actions into a reward.

## Moving the Goalpost

Moving the goalpost happens when you change expectations unexpectedly or at the last minute. A classic example is when two partners discuss housework. These conversations usually devolve into one partner feeling they are responsible for most of the chores. Let's say Craig and Chris are having the "Why aren't you doing enough?" conversation. Craig feels like he does most of the housework. Chris agrees to help more. One day, Chris proudly says he's done the laundry and dusted the apartment. Craig, wishing to be punitive, tells Chris that's great but asks why he didn't do the dishes as well.

Moving the goalposts makes your conversation partner feel off guard and implies no action they take will ever be good enough to satisfy your invisible goals. Progress in any conversation can never be made if you don't acknowledge that someone is trying and progressing toward a solution. In the above example, instead of moving a goalpost, Craig could have thanked Chris for the strides he has made.

## Oversimplification and Exaggeration

Oversimplification and exaggeration are two sides of the same manipulative coin. These strategies occur when an event's contributing factors are diminished or amplified so that the boundaries between causes and effects become indistinct or concealed. To put it differently, oversimplification occurs when multiple causes are condensed into one or a few reasons. In contrast, exaggeration arises when a small number of causes are magnified into numerous ones. Here are examples of both:

- "No one should be homeless. All the fast-food chains are hiring for $17 an hour." [Oversimplification]
- "All of these school shootings happen because everyone is on antidepressants and playing violent video games." [Overexaggeration]

In the first example, the speaker has painted a picture of homelessness being solely an employment issue. The reasons for homelessness are complex, and each individual's situation is unique. Affordable housing, divorce, domestic violence, drug addiction, and mental health issues are only a few factors that can contribute to homelessness.[41] However, this example does not take any of that into consideration and minimizes the issue to a single factor.

The second example claims that "everyone" is a medicated drone who plays *Call of Duty* twenty-four-seven. You're probably exaggerating whenever you say *everyone, every time, always,* or *never* in the middle of a courageous conversation. Unless you're discussing the immutable laws of physics or mathematics, there are few examples of anything being an everyone, no one, always, or never proposition. This is especially true when dealing with human behavior. In this example, millions of people take antidepressants and play video games. Not all those people own guns or will ever commit a violent act.

As much as oversimplification and exaggeration can be used to manipulate a courageous conversation, they're equally a trap for the well-intentioned. The desire to make sense of the world around us is a trait almost every human shares. Our brains are not supercomputers that can research or factor in every dynamic that contributes to an event, so we have a tendency to exaggerate or oversimplify to the point that that event makes sense to us. For example, you see someone run a red light and T-bone another vehicle. You might oversimplify the reason for the accident as the red-light runner not paying attention. That's a reasonable explanation for the accident. You didn't perceive the wasp that stung the driver or the oil slick in the middle of the intersection that made it difficult for both cars to brake.

When you find yourself straying into the territory of oversimplification or exaggeration, rely on curiosity to help get your conversation back on course. You're halfway home if you follow the rule that complex situations almost never have simple reasons or solutions. Every issue, from student debt to reproductive rights, is not simple or one-size-fits-all, and should never be approached as such. The rest of the way back on course is to ask, "What factors don't I know about that may contribute to this situation?" This is where curiosity kicks in. Find out what you don't know anytime you're about to make a blanket statement. I guarantee you'll be surprised at the results.

## Triangulation

Triangulation is when you literally or figuratively bring someone else's opinion into the conversation. I'm not talking about inserting a well-placed quote in a courageous conversation. The triangulation tactic pits your conversation partner's points of view against someone else's. In extremes, triangulation involves adding a third party to your conversation. "You know your mother disagrees with that. Why don't we give her a call?" is an example of sticking someone else's nose in your business, where it probably doesn't belong. Another form of triangulation brings authoritative, or pseudo-authoritative, sources into the conversation, specifically to discount someone else's truth. An example of this type of triangulation would be to cite fraudulent or irrelevant historical examples of how the Confederate flag stands for heritage, not hate, when your conversation partner simply expresses distress at seeing the Stars and Bars flying.

In either form of triangulation, the tactic is to beat your conversation partner down with numbers. It's more difficult to state your truth when people who disagree with you are added to the conversation or spurious facts are used to discount your experience. Guard against triangulation by being curious about your conversation partner's point of view. It doesn't always matter that you could line up a hundred people who would disagree with your conversation partner. What matters is that you take the time to understand your conversation partner's stance or feelings about a topic.

## Weaponizing Intent over Impact

Intent and impact are thorny topics when discussing courageous conversations. Intent is the point you wanted to get across, and impact is how the receiver of the message felt about what you said. There are two distinct situations where someone speaks about intent over impact. The first situation is intentionally misspeaking about something you should already know. Think of this like being introduced to someone a few times and still calling them the wrong name. Intentionally misspeaking can be hurtful when using the wrong pronouns, out-of-date/unacceptable terms, or anything else you've been told triggers your conversation partner. The second intent-over-impact gaffe is saying something you had no way of knowing would trigger someone. This is generally called foot-in-mouth disease. An example of foot in mouth is asking how someone's mom is doing and being informed she died a couple of weeks ago.

Weaponizing intent over impact has two common uses. The first is totally dismissing and not taking responsibility for what you said because "that wasn't my intent." The assumption is that because you didn't mean harm, your conversation partner should get over it, no matter how it made them feel. That defensive reaction makes sense from an emotional point of view. You've said something embarrassing and want to slide out of the consequences. But your words still hurt someone. How's that for impact?

The second weaponization of intent and impact is intentionally using words or phrases you know will get under someone's skin. "Oh, you baked that? It's actually good" is an example of an intentionally cutting comment. Slights or derogatory comments that relate to someone's identity are called microaggressions and fall into this category. Microaggressions are taunts that target your conversation partner's age, gender, sexual orientation, race, body type, or any other defining characteristic. If microaggressions are brought to light, the burden of responsibility is often placed on the receiver with a response like:

"Oh, you know I was just kidding."
"Why so thin-skinned?"
"Stop overreacting."

In either case of intentionally weaponizing intent and impact, the speaker is trying to gaslight the listener into believing there is something wrong with their reaction. Gaslighting is a subtle form of bullying used to sow self-doubt in someone's mind in order to get the upper hand in a courageous conversation. If you're thinking of weaponizing intent versus impact, please don't. Every instance I've ever come across, personally or professionally, is hurtful and will damage your relationship with your conversation partner.

## Emotional Regulation Is Freedom

When you get to the point where you can have a conversation and keep your emotions in check, you're free to choose how you respond. Nothing your conversation partner says, from personal attacks to outright falsehoods, holds any power over you. You are the ultimate arbiter of what you say and how you act. I would urge that, especially during courageous conversations, you hold on to your values. Being true to one set of values doesn't mean that you violate another set.

Let's say that truth and kindness are both parts of your value set, and your conversation partner says something you do not believe to be true. As we saw in the "How to Appreciate Someone's Message" section in the "Appreciating a Diversity of Opinion" chapter, not everyone's truth is the same. If your response to your conversation partner's perceived untruth is to be anything but kind, your value set is at odds. Use the techniques you've learned in this chapter to regulate your responses and fall in line with all your values.

If you're having problems aligning your emotional response with your values or your conversation partner says something out of bounds, here are a few responses to fall back on:

- "Thank you for sharing your opinions. I just wanted to express that this is a very triggering topic for me."
- "Can we please pause? What you just said triggered me, and I want to figure out why."

- "I value this conversation. However, I am feeling something right now and want to explore what it is before we continue. Would you mind giving me a few moments to collect my thoughts?"
- "Please give me some time to process what you are saying because I want to give you an appropriate response that's not based solely on my emotions."

No matter what your response is, you're making space to allow yourself time to remember that emotions are temporary and plan an appropriate emotionally regulated response. If that response has the potential to damage your relationship with your conversation partner, it's not the right response.

Emotional regulation isn't something you achieve overnight or without some work. Don't forget to use every emotionally charged situation as a laboratory to explore your emotional elevator. Every time you do so, it will get you closer to understanding yourself and how to better regulate your emotions. The following exercises and examples are designed to assist you in that endeavor. Above all else, when you experience strong emotions, take a breath and calm your mind. You've got this!

# Chapter 5—Exercises and Examples: Emotional Regulation

**Exercise**

I remember seeing an ad for an investment firm that included this disclaimer: "Past performance is not indicative of future returns." That sounded a little gloomy when applied to the stock market, but that statement is hopeful when applied to courageous conversations. If your past courageous conversations have been fraught with emotion, you can change that using the principles of EI and regulation.

The below worksheet builds on the Trigger Worksheet you completed in the last chapter. This time, I'd like you to think about courageous conversations where you displayed strong emotions linked to the topic. This worksheet aims to help you identify how different issues and your historical context to those topics evoke specific emotions. After identifying these potential pitfalls, you can develop strategies to regulate your emotional response whenever these topics arise. Here's a detailed explanation for each column.

- **Identify a courageous conversation topic**: The topics in this column should be specific enough to be actionable but not so specific you cannot easily plan for that type of conversation. For example, writing "the government" may be too vague to create an emotional regulation strategy. I'd suggest drilling down on that broad topic to a talking point like taxation or reproductive rights legislation.

- **Emotion(s) you feel about this courageous conversation topic**: Write down the strong emotion(s) that you feel about this topic. To help you catalog your feelings, I strongly suggest using emotions words such as *happiness, sadness, disgust, fear, surprise, exhaustion,* and *anger* in this column.[42] Feel free to utilize an emotion wheel, which is easily found on the web, to extend your emotional vocabulary. After you list the emotion, reflect on why you associate this emotion with this topic.

- **Historical context/proximity to this courageous conversation topic**: Record your historical context for this topic. Identify any personal associations with the topic. Look at it from every angle. Here are a few questions to guide you:
  - What were you taught about this topic?
  - How were you raised to think about this topic?
  - Were there any traumatic events associated with this topic?
  - How close in proximity are you to this topic?

  This level of reflection will help you better understand why this issue matters enough to you that it evokes emotion. If I were to record the topic of LGBTQIA+ rights in the first column, my historical context would be having two gay uncles and seeing their struggles. The more specific you can be with your historical context/proximity to the topic, the easier it will be for you to understand your emotional connection.

- **Triggers that you have or may have with this courageous conversation topic**: This column lists triggers, just like in the last chapter's exercise. Write down any triggers that you have had or could have related to this topic. If you need to examine a single trigger, use the worksheet from the "Triggers" chapter to assist you. As a result of my close proximity to the LGBTQIA+ community, I am more sensitive when a conversation partner is judgmental or uses derogatory or offensive references around this topic. This is the known trigger that can cause me to become very defensive and argumentative. It is my responsibility to understand that in order for me to self-regulate and be able to move out of the emotion and back to curiosity.

- **Proactive language to share with a conversation partner to address triggers**: The information in this column can be real or conjectural. If you have already successfully conveyed your trigger to your conversation partner, congratulations. Write down your success so it can be patterned for other topics. If you did not share your trigger, record what you could have said to let your conversation partner know the topic was emotionally triggering. Here are a few examples: With this knowledge, I proactively share my personal story with my conversation partner. I tell them that because of my intimate and personal proximity to the topic, I have a tendency to be a bit more sensitive when I hear certain things. However, I want to hear your thoughts and experiences.

Once you've written down five to ten different topics, look back over the list. Do you see any patterns emerge? Do you notice any topics that create a stronger emotional response? If that's the case, you can develop strategies to limit your response to that topic and emotion pairing. Like everything in the ACTER model, your strategies will take practice and intentional implementation to be successful.

| Identify a courageous conversation topic. (Example: divorce, gun rights, race, women's rights, etc.) | Describe the emotion(s) you feel about this courageous conversation topic. Why? | Historical context/ proximity to this courageous conversation topic. | Triggers that you have, or may have, with this courageous conversation topic. Why? | Proactive language to share with a conversation partner to address triggers. |
|---|---|---|---|---|
| | | | | |
| | | | | |
| | | | | |
| | | | | |
| | | | | |

## *Examples*

### Is It Time?

"She started meowing today and told me she was a cat."

Laila chuckled nervously and softly replied to her husband, Ted, "When I was seven, I wanted a cat, so I'd randomly meow to show Mom a cat wouldn't bother her. It made sense in my seven-year-old brain that meowing was a good litmus test for having a cat. Mom started meowing back to see if it would drive me nuts. It didn't, and we got a cat the next week."

"Honey, that's a cute story—but just now, she didn't know where she was or why she was meowing. It's fast approaching the point we're not going to be able to take care of her," said Ted in the kindest tone he could muster.

There was nothing kind in what Laila was hearing and thinking. Laila felt her face get flush, and her ears started ringing. Her husband's statement was throwing her into a mini rage as she thought: *How dare he. It's not that bad. Yes, Mom may slip a little from time-to-time, but we can handle it. We aren't putting my mom in one of those homes. We watched that* Dateline *special about Alzheimer's care homes. He saw how they warehouse people until they die. How could Ted be so callous?*

Ted knew his wife well enough to know that her silence was a good indication of how this conversation would end. The last time he'd mentioned care solutions for her mother, Laila got so angry at him that they barely spoke for a week. To be fair, Ted was a little heavy-handed when he last approached the topic. He thought he'd try a new tactic this time around.

"Honey, your mother is *our* responsibility. I love her too. I want her to get the best care possible, and neither of us is equipped to do that."

157

Laila knew Ted was right, but her feelings were getting in the way of rational thought. She mustered up the most adult thing she could think of and said, "I value this conversation. However, I am feeling something right now and want to explore what it is before we continue. Would you mind giving me a few moments to collect my thoughts?"

Ted nodded, and Laila rushed to the bathroom. She sat on the edge of the bathtub and cried for what felt like an hour. There came a point where her tears stopped. Laila knew she had to face the reality of her mother's mental degradation. Laila walked out of the bathroom and said to her husband, "Okay ... I might need to step away again, but I know we need to come up with a plan—together. This is so emotional for me. Let's talk about it."

## Coming Out

The knock on the bedroom door was almost inaudible, and Kevin called out, "Sam, is that you?"

"Yeah, you got a second, Dad?" said Sam.

"Come on in. Katherine and I are just reading," said Kevin.

Sam's father and stepmother put down their respective books and sat up in bed a little straighter as the sixteen-year-old boy crossed the room. The teenager sat down on the corner of the bed and looked at his dad without saying a word.

"What's going on, sport? How did dinner go with your mom?" Kevin asked.

"It was fine. I told her I wasn't going to be able to ask a girl to the homecoming dance," said Sam somberly.

"What? Surely, you're not scared to ask anyone out. I could give you some pointers ..." Kevin's voice trailed off as his wife chimed in.

"Like you've got any game," said Katherine.

That normally would have elicited a laugh from Sam, but the teen was silent. Kevin, oblivious to his son's unusual reaction, forged ahead, saying, "What about that girl in your trig class? She ..."

Katherine paused Kevin mid-sentence and put her hand on Kevin's arm, and said, "Sam. What's going on? You're not acting like yourself."

Sam lowered his head, paused for a second, and said, "I can't ask a girl to the dance because I'd rather ask a guy. I'm gay, and I can't live a lie anymore."

Within what felt like a microsecond, Kevin thought: *What? How can that be? He was always a little charmer. Gay? He's my only child. He's my only shot at grandkids. Is he really telling me he's gay? What does this mean? What about pronouns? Do I change what I call him—her—they? Why is this so confusing?*

Kevin needed a second to collect his thoughts. It wasn't that he was anti-gay. This was simply unexpected news. Speaking slowly and deliberately, Kevin said, "Sam, could you give me just a moment? My brain needs to catch up with what you just said."

Sam didn't look thrilled about having a delayed reaction from his dad, but the news was big. Having a minute or two pause was better than his dad doing the "no son of mine" rant.

Kevin took the time to catalog his emotions and to try to rationalize what was happening. *My son ... my only son, just came out to me, and my first thoughts were to make it about me. This is his life. And the world is horrible to gay people. What's going to happen to him? Is he going to get hurt by something someone does or says? I bet he's as scared as I am now. Say something, Kevin ...*

"Sam, I love you. Thank you for telling me. If that's who you are, I don't want you to feel like you're lying to the world. What do we do now? Do we throw a party? Do Kat and I ask a lot of awkward questions? Tell us what you need," said Kevin.

"You've already done it. Thank you, Dad. I love you too. And please, no awkward questions," said Sam.

Then Kevin and Katherine got out of bed, hugged their boy, and proceeded to spend the next hour asking him awkward questions.

## CHAPTER 6

# R—Respectful Listening

The final step in the ACTER model is R—Respectful Listening. While it is one of the most important components of the framework, it is often the most ignored. Usually, in a day-long session, we get to the respectful listening section right as the after-lunch carb crash happens. Some of the participants' eyes glaze over, and I can tell they're thinking: *Respectful listening? My ears are open, and I can hear what's being said. I'm good on this step.* Respectful listening isn't just being present while trying to catch the Cliff's Notes version of what your conversation partner is saying. That level of listening might be good enough to absorb chit-chat or minor instructions, but it doesn't cut it when discussing why the in-laws are coming to town and staying at the house instead of getting a hotel room.

As corny as it might sound, respectful listening means listening with your heart. In this chapter, you'll learn how to become more of an empathetic listener, how to create a favorable listening environment, and how some courageous conversation partners give unexpected clues related to their moods. Some of the material in this chapter will sound familiar to you. We've discussed various listening techniques throughout this book. Let this serve as a reminder that many of the skills that make up the steps of the ACTER model are interconnected. Where possible, in this chapter, I've noted where we've previously mentioned skills. You may find it helpful to refer to those sections to strengthen your understanding of these points.

## Active Listening Versus Respectful Listening

In the "Curiosity" chapter, you learned how to engage your conversation partner with open-ended questions. (If you need a refresher on that, go back to the "Phrases of Curiosity" and "How to Engage with Curiosity" sections of that chapter.) Using open-ended questions is part of a skill set called active listening. You've already been exposed to several active listening techniques throughout this book. Below is a list of active listening skills. These skills were covered in previous chapters, but it's handy to have all of the listening skills in one place. If you need to refer to those sections, feel free to take the time to do so.

- Listen without taking a position or making judgments. Remember, your goal in any courageous conversation is to gain insight into your conversation partner's positions. ("Curiosity Is the Opposite of Judgment" section of the "Curiosity" chapter.)
- Focus on your conversation partner's message by making eye contact and repeating every sentence your conversation partner says in your mind before speaking. If you think you missed something, ask your conversation partner to repeat

their last statement. ("Selective Perception" section of the "Appreciating Diversity of Opinion" chapter.)

- Ask open-ended questions when you don't understand your conversation partner's intent, or you need additional information. ("Phrases of Curiosity" section of the Curiosity chapter.) Ask, "Let me see if I understand this," and repeat what your conversation partner said in your own words. If you didn't understand, or their statement evokes an emotional response, ask for a moment to reflect on their statement and try again. ("How to Appreciate Someone's Message" section of the "Appreciating Diversity of Opinions" chapter and "Emotional Regulation is Freedom" section of the "Emotional Regulation" chapter.)

Each of the active listening skills is designed to gather the facts about your conversation partner or the basis of their opinions. Curiosity through active listening techniques is necessary to build trust and understanding between conversation partners. If you only gather information, you'll miss a huge component of what your conversation partner is trying to convey. To get to the other-than-information part of the conversation, we'll need to use a different skill set: respectful listening.

The difference between active and respectful listening is much like the difference between intelligence and wisdom we discussed in the "Emotional Regulation" chapter. Active listening is gathering facts (intelligence), and respectful listening is effectively interpreting what's being said (wisdom). Respectful listening transcends the words being said and takes into account nonverbal communication, such as your conversation partners. Considering your conversation partner's tone, timing, speed of speech, body language, and cultural/historical contexts are all elements of respectful listening.

Some of the elements of respectful listening are intertwined with our perspective, and you use them instinctively. Unless you've missed a conversational cue, you can feel when the winds of a conversation blow in a different direction. During a courageous conversation, have you ever said, for no other reason than a gut feeling:

"You sound upset."
"You got mad all of a sudden. What did I say?"
"You're quiet. What's wrong?"

In each of these examples, you've tapped into the emotional state of your conversation partner without your conversation partner telling you what their emotional state is.

## Levels of Listening

There are few metrics that you can use in the ACTER model. How do you quantify appreciation of diversity or personal curiosity? There's no objective way to see how well you're doing in these areas other than the outcomes of your courageous conversations. But unlike the other ACTER model steps, we can rank how well we're listening on the following three-level scale.

**Level 1: You are passively hearing.** There is a difference between listening and hearing. Hearing is something we passively do without energy or effort. Hearing is involuntary. You hear whether you want to or not. You can probably hear what background noises or sounds are happening around you right now. On the other hand, listening is active and requires attention and intention. When we listen, we actively put meaning to the sounds and words we hear. At Level 1, you hear your conversation partner, but your ability to listen to them is limited. This is often because your emotions are high and unregulated. Your focus is on responding to the driving emotion and stating your point of view. Even when your conversation partner does speak, your responses are all about how it pertains to your thoughts, feelings, and opinions. Your tendency to interrupt more and make topics about yourself is greater. Judgmental and defensive listening happens at Level 1.

**Level 2: You are listening but with a motive.** You are engaged and mindful of the conversation with the other person. You are committed to hearing what is being said. You engage in conversation without hostility but still bring strong emotions and beliefs to the table and focus the conversation on making your point. When we approach a conversation from this mindset, we call it a *discussion*. In a discussion, our goal is still more focused on persuasion and presenting our ideas. Emotions are not taken into account, and questions are usually used as a tactic to push an agenda.

**Level 3: You are actively listening with empathy and curiosity.** You're focused on regulating your emotions and placing energy and intention toward sincerely seeking to understand your conversation partner by actively listening. You choose to step outside your own experiences, listen to their words, and ask thoughtful questions to detect underlying meaning, thinking, values, and feelings. You acknowledge and verbally reflect on the other person's feelings and experiences. You show empathy by affirming the other person's experience. You show respect for the other person and their experience and opinion, even if you do not share it.[43] When we approach a conversation from this mindset, we call it *dialogue*. The goal of a dialogue is to share ideas to broaden our perspective.

At Level 1 Listening, nothing is more important than protecting your beliefs, worldview, and experiences. Your conversational mindset at Level 1 is either win-lose or lose-lose, and you're demonstrating a fixed mindset. (Refer back to the "Conversation Goals" and "Fixed and Growth Mindsets" sections of the "How to Use this Book" chapter for those definitions.) Level 1 Listening is the mental equivalent of war. Emotions are high, and you have dug your feet into the sand. You're defensive, and anything your conversation partner says that does not agree with your perspective means you're ready to react. Your behavior is more combative, and all of your mental energy is expended on listening with the intent to respond. You are also more focused on yourself and your needs, so much so that your inner monologue drowns out what your conversation partner says. Level 1 Listening can occur when we are emotionally triggered and feel emotions such as anger, rage, defensiveness, or frustration. When we approach a conversation from this mindset, we call it a *debate*. A debate is focused on winning, and hearing is minimized. We tend to focus only on defending our opinions and a single perspective.

Remember, high emotions cancel out logical thinking. When emotions are this high, harmful behaviors are more likely. Level 1 listening during conversations isn't having a conversation at all. It's more like each person is playing solitaire. Even if the conversation is important, realize that listening at this level won't bring about anything fruitful. If you find yourself being a Level 1 listener, it should be used as a signal to tell you to go back to the ACTE of the ACTER Model. It is okay to pause to allow for emotions to subside. Find a way to get the conversation back on track by being open to hearing the different perspectives of your conversation partner, being curious, identifying what triggered you, and regulating your emotions. If that doesn't work, politely end the conversation. There's no use speaking when no one is listening anyway.

If you're at Listening Level 2, emotions are not the primary driver, and you're practicing active listening skills, but for an ulterior motive. Level 2 listening is the equivalent of double Dutch. Yes, you are listening, and you're letting your conversation partner speak, but you are just waiting to jump in. You're focused on your conversation partner's message and are fully present because you need to identify rebuttal points. Any pause in their sentence feels like an opportunity to take a turn. At this listening level, your conversation partner does at least feel like a part of the conversation or that they can make their point and be heard. There is a catch with Level 2 listening—you're still intent on making your point. You're following the Golden Rule because you want to be heard too. Some Level 2 listeners may be involved in a lose-win conversational mindset. That's where your conversation partner is agreeable to being liked or accepted. Here's an example of what a Level 2 conversation can sound like:

"Has the research team been working out for you? I've had some issues with them not getting things in on time recently."

"They've been working out great for me. I developed a new macro to filter their findings. You can see how it's organized here."

"That looks great. I can see how that macro helped filter the data points. Good job! But where's the final analysis?"

"Oh, it's down here."

"Yeah … that's way out of whack. I'm not sure the research team got everything we needed. Tell me exactly what they gave you, and did they get it in on time?"

In this Level 2 conversation, the first speaker is more interested in grinding their axe with the research team than looking at a new data analysis method. The first speaker is complimentary of the second speaker's work, but it's only a means to an end. Unfortunately, most conversations are Level 2. When you focus more on angling to satisfy your agenda than being curious about your conversation partner's experiences, perspective, and needs, you're missing half of the conversation. Remember, the goal of any courageous conversation is to gather information about your conversation partner and their position. You can't fully achieve that goal when looking for personal gain.

Level 3 listening is what you're striving for. Listening at Level 3 is the ultimate form of curiosity. When you listen at Level 3, you approach the conversation with an open mind and a goal to broaden your perspective and find shared meaning. To do that, you are intentional about being keenly aware of the diverse perspectives and needs of yourself and your conversation partner. In Level 3 Listening, judgment is blocked by pure curiosity. Every question is grounded in the intent to understand. Your focus is keen, and you constantly take inventory to get a feel for what's happening in the conversation by using all your senses. Level 3 listening uses body language, tone of voice, and choice of wording to interpret your conversation partner's message. If you're walking into a courageous conversation, Level 3 listening allows you to read the room's emotional state by analyzing nonverbal cues.

Not to sound too woo-woo, but at Level 3, you're not listening to understand someone's words. You're trying to tap into the energy behind their words. Empathy is present in Level 3 Listening.

Here's an example of a Level 3 conversation:

Donna walks into the break room, constantly looking at her phone. She slides her thumb down the phone's screen every few seconds as if refreshing an app. Lisa greets Donna with a simple hello and ask how her day is going.

"Uhm ... it's going fine," Donna says without looking up from her phone.

Usually, Donna is a chatterbox, and her noncommittal tone is out of character. Concerned, Lisa stops Donna, probes a little to find out what's happening, and asks, "No, seriously, is everything ok? You seem a little distracted today."

"No, my son's school just went on lockdown, and I can't contact him or anyone at the school. I'm trying not to panic. Why does this keep happening?" said Donna.

"Oh, Donna, I am so sorry. You must be worried sick. How can I help? What is the number of the school? I can call, and maybe we could double your chances of getting through to someone," said Lisa.

Lisa uses every form of listening available in this example. Lisa sees Donna's body language and pairs that with Donna's usual behavior to ascertain something is amiss. You can't get much more curious about someone than that. Level 3 listening doesn't happen automatically. Like everything else in the ACTER model, there are ancillary skills you must develop to help you reach Level 3. The following few sections will teach you strategies and skills to improve your listening game.

## Location, Location, Location

One of the hidden elements of respectful listening, and a skill you'll need to achieve Level 3, is choosing an environment conducive to having a courageous conversation. That concept might sound like a no-brainer. For example, you'd never start a conversation about a sensitive personal matter on a crowded bus. Unfortunately, you don't always get to schedule courageous conversations ahead of time. Many courageous conversations are circumstantial and when they start is outside of your control.

Let's say your buddy invited you to hear their Pink Floyd cover band. You love Pink Floyd, so you make your way to a dive bar on a Tuesday night to listen to them play. For two excruciating hours, the band belts the loudest and cringe-worthiest "artistic interpretations" of song after song of one of your favorite artists. At the end of the set, your friend jumps off the stage and is beaming. In his mind, he's just been inducted into the Rock and Roll Hall of Fame. Then he asks you, "What did you think?"

Standing in the middle of the bar when your friend is on top of the world isn't the time or place to have this courageous conversation. If you want to practice respectful listening, you'll need to put a pin in the conversation for a later time and better place by saying something like: "Thank you for inviting me out tonight. I'm glad I could be a part of your performance." A couple of days later, when your friend's emotions aren't running so high, you pick a time and place best suited to give him open, honest, yet kind feedback.

Courageous conversations often turn sour because we get sucked into a wrong place, wrong time situation like the one above. If you are not in a place that will allow you to achieve a Level 3, try to delay the conversation until you can get somewhere that you can. Changing a conversation's venue isn't always possible, but be aware that it's sometimes a possibility. As long as you're not using this as an avoidance technique, you can reschedule a courageous conversation by saying something like one of the following:

"That's a little more in-depth than we have time for in this department head meeting. Can we schedule a one-on-one to discuss this further?"

"I want us to be able to give each other our full attention, and this noisy coffee shop probably isn't that place. Can we finish this discussion when we get home?"

"I'd rather not have this conversation over the phone. Are you free now or sometime today? I can come over, and let's talk about this."

The final example is where I believe we set ourselves up for failure in a courageous conversation the most—electronic communications. When we have conversations via phone, text, or email, the following communication theory claims we can lose as much as 93 percent of the meaning our conversation partner is trying to get across. In the late 1960s, behavioral psychologist Dr. Albert Mehrabian came up with the 7-38-55 rule that breaks down how we interpret face-to-face conversations: 7 percent verbal, 38 percent voice and tone, and 55 percent body language.[44] You and your conversation partner are missing over half of the elements needed for full understanding by speaking on the phone. You may be able to get to Level 2 on a phone call. Communicating via text or email is a Level 1 proposition at best. If a conversation matters, do yourself a favor and have it face-to-face.

When picking a favorable environment for a courageous conversation, consider the following guidelines:

- Choose a place that is private and quiet. A closed office, living room, or anywhere that limits the number of people around is best. Turn off all TVs, radios, and cell phone notifications to limit distractions.
- If possible, arrange seating so you and your conversation partner have equal height and comfortable seats that are no more than ten feet apart. Be mindful of desks or coffee tables that are positioned between you and your conversation partner. Psychologically speaking, having physical barriers creates subliminal mental barriers between conversation participants.
- The time of day matters when having courageous conversations. Most people on traditional work/sleep cycles are most alert and happiest between 10 AM and noon. Try to time courageous conversations at work during these hours. The afternoon lunch crash time around 2 PM should be avoided at all costs.[45] For personal conversations, try after an early dinner and not too close to the bedtime, a window of 6 PM to 8 PM.
- Get in the habit of using text messages and email for informational purposes only. Anything with more emotional content than "let's meet at seven" or "pick up eggs" can be easily misunderstood.

Of course, these rules describe ideal circumstances. If there's no choice but to have a courageous conversation in less perfect conditions, try to maximize the effects of the 7-38-55 rule. Is there anything you can do, given where you're having the conversation, to increase how well you can hear your conversation partner's tone or see their body language? If you're having a conversation while taking a walk around the park, try to look at your conversation partner frequently in order to pick up on their body language.

## Understanding Nonverbal Communications

Now that you've created a setting conducive to Level 3 listening, you must interpret the parts of the 7-38-55 rule correctly. Unless someone uses specialized vocabulary you're unfamiliar with, you should be able to easily understand the verbal portion of the 7-38-55 rule. It's the other 93 percent of nonverbal communications you may need help with. Just because our perspective clues us in to some aspects of nonverbal communication, you can't solely rely on your life experiences to be an infallible guide. For example, cultural differences can significantly affect how nonverbal communication should be interpreted and may not be part of your life's lexicon. The best practice here is to set baseline definitions and strategies to give you the best chance at Level 3 interactions.

Predictably, nonverbal communication, also known as nonverbal cues, conveys information without using words. These cues include facial expressions, body language, tone of voice, and gestures. These cues can greatly influence the interpretation of the message being conveyed. To make matters more complicated, nonverbal cues can reinforce or contradict the verbal message and even communicate messages that are entirely different from the spoken words.

One of my favorite examples of contradictory verbal and nonverbal communication is someone saying, "I'm fine." Interpreting the meaning of the words only as they have been spoken relays a message of being happy, satisfied with your present situation, or generally content. You probably know from past experiences that taking the statement "I'm fine" at face value is a perilous prospect. The nonverbal cues attached to "I'm fine" relay the phrase's exact meaning. Depending on what those cues are, "I'm fine" can mean anything from happiness to being so mad you can't quite see straight. If you've never been on the wrong side of interpreting "I'm fine," consider yourself lucky.

The way to crack the "I'm fine" code is by correctly interpreting the speaker's tone and speed of voice. One's vocal inflections and timbre can convey a wide range of emotions. Someone speaking in unusually low vocal tones can denote anger or frustration. A high-pitched voice can indicate excitement or nervousness. An even monotone voice can convey boredom or disinterest. The pace and rhythm of speech can also carry meaning. A fast vocal pace indicates urgency or excitement, while a slow pace can indicate thoughtfulness or contemplation.

Sometimes, vocal tones aren't enough to decipher a statement's meaning, and you should turn to your conversation partner's facial expressions for insight. Facial expressions can convey a wide range of emotions, from happiness and contentment to anger and frustration. For example, a smile can indicate pleasure, while a frown can indicate sadness or disapproval. Eye contact is another crucial aspect of nonverbal communication, and it can convey confidence, sincerity, and attentiveness.

Body language is another important aspect of nonverbal communication. This can include posture, hand gestures, and the movement of the body. For example, leaning forward can indicate interest or engagement, while crossing one's arms can indicate defensiveness or hostility. Hand gestures can also convey meaning, such as pointing to indicate direction or waving to indicate greeting.

All of these nonverbal cues are influenced by cultural factors. Different cultures have different norms and nonverbal communication expectations. What's considered appropriate in one culture may be inappropriate in another. Going back to eye contact, locking gazes is often seen as a sign of respect in Western cultures. In some Asian cultures, on the other hand, avoiding eye contact can be a sign of respect. If you didn't know the cultural difference between Western and Asian body language styles, you could assume that by not making eye contact, your Asian counterpart was being deceptive. Western cultures often wrongly associate eye avoidance with deception.[46] Imagine the mess you could get yourself in if your Asian conversation partner was trying to honor you by not making eye contact and you assumed they were lying to you. Additionally, hand gestures that are innocuous in one culture may be offensive or even insulting in another. In the United States, wagging your index finger in the come-here gesture is acceptable in most circumstances. If you make that same gesture in the Philippines, it's akin to flipping the bird.

I'd urge you to remember that cultural differences aren't only defined by a country's borders, racial makeups, or geographic regions. Cultural differences can happen between neighborhoods in the same town or even between various departments in the same company. If you're unsure of what is appropriate to say or do in an unfamiliar situation—watch, ask, and learn. You'll figure it out if you just listen.

# Honoring Diversity Through Listening

Coming full circle in the ACTER model, we started the discussion with diversity, and we'll end with diversity. In the context of listening, diversity means applying your Level 3 listening skills to those who have a different race, gender, socioeconomic status, culture, lifestyle, experience, or interest than you. When you listen at Level 3, you respect the differences you have with your conversation partner as their unique perspectives—not as a way to be divisive. When you listen, you not only understand the thoughts and feelings of others, but you also build stronger connections with them. It's harder to misinterpret how someone thinks or feels when we don't have to guess or rely on our biases to fill in the blanks.

When you listen to someone, you show them that you value their thoughts and opinions. This can help to create a sense of belonging and trust, which is crucial for building strong relationships. You can find common ground and shared experiences that help us to connect with others if you take the time to listen. This connection can create a sense of unity, which can help take the stress out of courageous conversations. As with all the skills you've learned in the ACTER model, respectful listening takes habit and practice. The exercises and examples in this chapter's section will help you achieve Level 3 listening and confirm your commitment to a diversity of opinion.

# Chapter 6—Exercises and Examples: Respectful Listening

## Exercise

In my classes, the exercise I use is a role-playing session to reinforce the lessons of respectful listening. I have the participants get in groups of three and give them a topic to discuss. One participant is in favor of the topic, one is against it, and the third person is an observer. The "for" and "against" participants must each discuss their side of the topic for three minutes. The goal for each person is to achieve a listening level 3 during the conversation, and the observer grades the participants' performance. After the observer critiques the discussion, everyone rotates roles. If you have two friends willing to participate in this role-playing exercise, I strongly suggest that you take advantage of this training.

You can expand role-playing exercises beyond critiquing listening levels if you have the time and a group of friends interested in improving their communication skills. You can practice each part of the ACTER model using "for" and "against" roleplay. After each three-minute session, all the participants should discuss elements of the ACTER model they witnessed and employed. Sharing how you felt you were utilizing the ACTER model will give your compatriots ideas about how they can improve their techniques. Talking about using the ACTER model is especially important with the internalized elements like triggers and emotional regulation. Your other participants will have no idea what's hit a nerve or how you kept your cool unless you tell them.

If you cannot get a group together, the following examples can also be used as solo exercises. These scenarios reflect shifts between all three levels of listening. As you read through the conversations, identify which level of listening each participant has achieved. The level of listening is in brackets at the end of each person's statements. Consider how you might approach each step of these conversations differently as a bonus exercise.

### *Examples*

#### No Promotion for You

"Laura, this conversation isn't going to be easy. But it's not for the reasons you'll initially think," said Maria.

Laura pounced on her boss's slight pause and said, "So I didn't get the promotion." [Level 1]

"No, I'm sorry you didn't. But—"

Laura wouldn't let up on her boss and fired back, "Three months ago, you called me into this office and told me that if I showed you more leadership skills, the team lead position was pretty much mine. Do you know—" [Level 1]

Maria wouldn't let this conversation get off the rails and interjected, "I know how much you've stepped up. I know how much overtime you've put in. Is there some area of your performance that I might not be aware of?" [Level 2]

Laura replied, "I'm sorry for getting snappy. I ... I just thought I had the job. And you should know everything I've been doing. I went to great lengths to inform you so I could get the job. I cut you off earlier. Could you please continue?" [Level 2]

"Laura, I know you're upset. But I want to reinforce that you're a valued member of my team. I know you think that's a load of bologna since you didn't get the promotion. But there are reasons

178

I didn't pick you for this job," said Maria, waiting to see if Laura was ready for a productive dialogue. [Level 3]

"Do you have time to discuss those reasons now? We have such a great working relationship, so I know there must be very valid reasons why I didn't get the promotion," said Laura. [Level 3]

"There are, and you're going to think this is me trying to diffuse your feelings, but it's not. You're not a good fit to lead this team. It's not because you're not qualified. You're so incredibly adept at the technical side of our platforms you wouldn't be able to develop yourself further fully. Also, our team is relatively young. I can tell your heart lies in creating technical solutions. Your passion isn't developing people. I want to help you be where you'll be happiest and most effective." [Level 3]

Laura thought for a moment, and realized her boss was right. Over the last three months, everything Laura brought to her boss's attention was efficiencies she found in a process or a new feature of the company's software. Maybe it was time for Laura to reevaluate what she wanted to be when she grew up.

"What does that look like? Me moving to the development team or some other department? Will that impact you and this team? I've got so many questions. Thank you for this," said Laura. [Level 3]

## Customer Complaint

"I'm not sure why I've been bounced to you, but you're the third person I'll have spoken with in the last hour. Do you all even talk to each other or, let me guess, start from the beginning and tell you what the issue is—again?" [Level 1]

Justin had just returned from lunch and had no idea who the caller was or how they got through to his desk. He normally didn't deal with clients unless he was doing a site check or in a planning meeting. He certainly wasn't in the mood to catch an earful, but there was no need to escalate the situation.

"Hi, I'm Justin, and I'm one of the engineers. I'm sorry, but I don't know what's going on. I just returned from lunch, but I would be happy to help if possible." [Level 2]

"I don't know why when you folks screwed up this order, I've got to waste my time repeating myself. If it wasn't for the fact your company designed our assembly line's conveyor belt systems and all the parts are proprietary, I'd use someone else," said the terse voice on the phone. [Level 1]

"Okay, now we're getting somewhere. I'm one of the engineers that design those custom systems. I can also guess that since you're pretty upset, you had to order a replacement part, and we sent you the wrong thing. You'll lose a day's production because you think we're incompetent. Am I getting close?" asked Justin. [Level 3]

"That's about right, yes," said the still-unnamed voice on the phone.

"We're not incompetent, but mistakes do happen. I'd also bet there's a good reason you were put in contact with me. Let's start with who you are, what company you're with, what problem you were trying to solve, and what part you ordered," said Justin. [Level 2]

For the next fifteen minutes, Justin listened intently to the caller, Davi. Justin was correct: a control box on Davi's assembly line was hit by a forklift and needed to be replaced. The problem was that the control box's wiring harness wasn't the correct configuration to plug into the assembly line's motors. Both Davi and Justin were baffled because everything else matched up. Purchase order requests, shipping logs, and even the assembly line's schematics called for the part that was ordered and shipped.

"I don't get it. That control box should work. The guys in production and shipping are top-notch. They don't make mistakes." said Justin. [Level 1]

"You sound as frustrated as I do. Tell you what, let me send you a picture of the control box we have and the control box we received. That might help you figure out what's going on. Give me your email," said Davi. [Level 3]

A few moments later, Justin's email alert sounded. When he compared the pictures of the two control boxes, he knew exactly what was going on.

"I've got it. The control box part number was written down wrong on the schematic. You ordered the right thing. We shipped the right thing. Your system was installed a few years before I got here, but I'll get you an updated parts list. I can get you up and running in a few minutes if you have a screwdriver and a soldering iron ..." [Level 3]

True to his word, Justin walked Davi through changing out the wiring harness, and the assembly line was up and running within the hour.

_____

_____

_____

_____

_____

_____

_____

_____

_____

_____

_____

_____

_____

_____

_____

_____

_____

_____

_____

_____

_____

# Conclusion

The goal of this book is to help you have courageous conversations from an emotionally intelligent lens. Everyone from Confucius to Tom Hanks has been quoted as saying, "If it was easy, everyone would do it." It doesn't matter who the originator of that statement was. There's truth in that simple sentence. If having courageous conversations or diving headlong into divergent opinions were as easy as making a bowl of breakfast cereal, the world would be a harmonious place—but it's not. Most of the world avoids courageous conversations at all costs. You've taken a different path that puts you in the crosshairs of differences and discomfort, all for the sake of growth and understanding. Congratulations to you for doing the "not easy" thing. There are a thousand tiny bits of advice and strategies I wish I could give you before you have your next courageous conversation. My editor wouldn't be too happy with me if I had a thousand-point list, so I'm sure she'll settle for my top three bits of advice.

First, look for opportunities to limit the need for courageous conversations by opening dialogues when you see problems ahead. It's much easier to have a conversation about an issue that's not yet a problem but very well could be than to have a courageous conversation about a sore subject. Like going to the dentist or cleaning out your gutters, proactive conversations are never something you want to do, but in the end they save you from future headache or heartache.

I have a colleague whom I also count as a friend. She does free-lance work for me occasionally, and she's had phenomenal success over the years. She's grown her brand to the point that she's hired a virtual assistant. Recently, that assistant sent out an introductory email reminding everyone of my friend's office hours and the need to schedule appointments for *all* calls and meetings.

Working with someone with whom you have a friendship and a professional relationship isn't always easy. You have to be mindful of boundaries in both aspects of the relationship. My initial instinct was to shoot her a text asking what that message meant for me and how we should communicate. I realized that was not the best way to have that conversation. So the next time we had coffee, I asked her if I needed to make appointments to speak with her during business hours or text her as I've always done. My query wasn't designed to be an "Oh, Miss Big Shot has a virtual assistant. Do you have time for your friends?" comment. I know how busy she is, so I genuinely wanted to respect her time and define our work/friendship guidelines. She understood my intent and told me she was swamped and personal texts were fine during work hours. If we need to talk about a project or even personal stuff that may take a while, it is best to make an appointment or wait to talk after work. That simple question relieved her of having a future courageous conversation with me, defining her personal and professional boundaries.

Let's assume that in an alternate universe I didn't ask my friend to clarify her boundaries and continued to go off our usual patterns. I continued calling about work projects and personal stuff. Well, after a few months of this, one fateful day, I picked up the phone to share some personal news, and it was 100 percent the wrong day to do so. My friend didn't have the time to speak with me, and she decided it was time to tell me that I should have made an appointment with her assistant. That's a difficult conversation to have with a friend. I'm sure that discussion would have been emotionally charged and given us both needless stress on a busy day.

Proactive conversations take the same mindsets and courage you've learned with the ACTER model. Your goal with proactive conversations is the same as with any courageous conversation—to gather information about your conversation partner. Present the topic you foresee as an issue and let your conversation partner speak. For some conversations, you might find that your conversation partner isn't ready or doesn't see the need for the conversation at that time. Their feelings are perfectly valid, and you should not press the issue. Let them know the topic is important to you. Give your conversation partner time to wrap their mind around the subject and ask them to let you know when they're ready to revisit it.

My second tip is that while you should always strive for excellence in all your endeavors, flawless execution 100 percent of the time isn't realistic. You will become involved in unexpected courageous conversations with a difficult conversation partner who will frustrate you to the point where you'll forget the steps of the ACTER model. I've been involved in courageous conversations where I couldn't explain why I held on to a point with bleeding hands. The truth is, we're human, and we all have bad days. Give yourself grace and mercy. Remember, this is not about perfection. It's about continuous growth. If you don't show up at your best, it's okay to fall back, lick your wounds, and converse again another day.

When you fall short, the grace you give yourself should also be freely given to your conversation partner. This wouldn't be a proper communications/self-help book if it didn't include Maya Angelou's quote, "Do the best you can until you know better. Then, when you know better, do better."[47] That sentiment applies not only to you but also to how you view your interactions with your conversation partners. If you're having a good-faith conversation with someone, help them do better by not being critical of minor missteps. Your conversation partner is likely trying to do better but might not be in the same place you are. Here's an example:

"I talked to Alison yesterday, and she thought the same thing you do."

"I'll have to talk to them about that."

"Them? I was only talking about Alison."

"Oh, Alison uses they/them pronouns."

"Thank you for letting me know. I'm trying to get the hang of the pronoun thing, but changing lifetime habits is hard. I'll be sure to use they and them when speaking with them in the future."

If you're looking for a reason to shut a courageous conversation down, being judgmental or taking umbrage to small mistakes is a wonderful way to go. I see this happen all the time in online conversations. A poster searches for meaning or clarification of a complex topic but uses a single out-of-date term or phrase. Inevitably, the original question is thrown to the wayside, and the poster is flamed for using that single term or phrase. It's possible to help someone else understand that our language and definitions are changing quickly. Not everyone got the memo that certain terms are now offensive. Be kind to those trying to do better and help them along the way. Then, go back to your initial conversation and be curious about what your conversation partner thinks and feels.

I'm not suggesting that you accept or slough off harsh language, verbal abuse, or violations of preset boundaries. There's a considerable difference between misusing someone's pronouns and a curse word-laden rant. Once your conversation partner crosses that Rubicon, the conversation needs to end immediately. You should let your conversation partner know why you're stopping the conversation and literally walk away. Here are a few phrases that will help you end an icky conversation:

"I don't like it when you talk to me like that."

"My feelings get hurt when you say _____."

"I don't appreciate being cursed at."

"That comment doesn't sit well with me."

"I feel unnecessarily criticized when you say _____."

"Comments like that are offensive and make me feel bad about myself."

If this conversation happened in a professional setting, document the conversation as soon as possible. Then immediately let your boss or someone in your human resources department know what happened. I'd urge you not to allow instances of verbal abuse go by telling yourself your conversation partner was "having a bad day" or "is normally a good person." Both of those conditions may be true, but it's likely that your unacceptable conversation with this person isn't an isolated incident. You and your work colleagues deserve to work in an environment free from abusive or hurtful behaviors.

There is a big difference between an uncomfortable conversation and an abusive conversation. Verbal abuse is as destructive as other types of abuse. Over time, verbal abuse will make you doubt your self-worth, make you feel insecure, and will get worse or more intense. If you're unsure of what verbal abuse looks like, here are some of the forms it can take:

- **Criticism:** Persistent reminders that you or your actions are never good enough. Criticism is generally paired with moving the goalposts, so you can never succeed.
- **Sarcasm:** Cutting duplicitous statements and attitudes that make you unsure of what is a real statement and what's derision. Excessive sarcasm can also be a form of gaslighting.
- **Put-downs:** Repeated insults and attacks about any conceivable topic—from the way you dress to how you perform menial tasks.
- **Shaming:** Statements or questions designed to create feelings of internal disgust or question your self-worth. "What's the matter with you?" or "What were you thinking?" are common shaming questions.
- **Name-calling:** Insults disguised as pet names, swearing. [48]

Verbal abuse isn't limited to a parent-child or partner relationship. Your best friend could be verbally abusive toward you, and it is just as damaging as if a spouse was abusive. If you think you're in a verbally abusive relationship, please seek help. The Day One Hotline (1-866-223-1111) provides phone help for victims of verbal abuse. That's Not Cool also has a twenty-four-hour hotline (1-866-331-9474 or 1-866-331-8453 TTY) that can guide you to other organizations that could be a right fit for you.[49]

My final big tip is to remember that ACTER is a model. Conversations don't always follow a well-defined agenda. You won't necessarily be able to start a conversation appreciating your conversation partner's different opinions and end with respectful listening. The ACTER model is more of a conversational toolbox than a precise blueprint. Use the parts of the ACTER model as the conversation dictates. Below, I've given you two examples of a conversation that follows the ACTER model step by step and another one that bounces around the steps.

# A Courageous Conversation Using the ACTER Model Sequentially

"Wow, I am so sad that the Supreme Court ended affirmative action in universities," said Alisha.

"I'm not. Everyone should be admitted based on their qualifications and merits," replied Paul.

###  A (Appreciating Diversity of Opinion)

"Okay, I can appreciate that point of view, Paul. I've honestly not had this conversation with many people before, but especially not with a white man, so I am interested in hearing your opinion," said Alisha.

Paul agreed and replied, "You and I have been friends and colleagues for a while, so I would love to hear your thoughts on this topic. I am always curious about the other side's thoughts, but I never had the courage to talk to anyone about it. I don't want to say the wrong thing or ruin a friendship. But I think a good dialogue around this topic may give us both something new to consider."

 ## C (Curiosity)

"I do not think affirmative action is needed, but what are your thoughts, Alisha?" asked Paul.

Well, when it comes to what you said about affirmative action, I agree with you. All students *should* be admitted to universities based on their qualifications and merits. The challenge is history has shown us that that is not the case. Minorities have blatantly been discriminated against for years, and affirmative action aimed to minimize that and ensure somewhat of an even playing field. With such a deep history and continuation of discrimination against minorities, why do you think affirmative action is not needed?" replied Alisha.

 ## T (Trigger)

"I just don't think affirmative action is fair. It's nothing but reverse discrimination. Race should not be a factor in college admissions. I feel like it undermines the principle of meritocracy by prioritizing race over qualifications and merits," said Paul.

"Paul, it is hard for me to hear complaints about fair treatment come from the mouth of a white man. That was not fair. Let me start over. I think this is a huge topic with a deep-rooted history that has multiple factors that need to be considered. As a black woman, do you think that I want to be selected for anything JUST because I am a minority? No! However, I also understand that there was and still is a strong need for implementing affirmative action because discrimination against minorities happens. Unfortunately, it was implemented to address ongoing racial disparities and to create an equal opportunity and playing field for minorities who had historically been denied access based on race."

"So, to end discrimination, the solution is to discriminate? That makes no sense, Alisha, and you know it," said Paul.

Alisha replied, "But discrimination and taking race into consideration was perfectly fine when it was for white people during slavery and Jim Crow."

"That is not fair, Alisha. You're comparing apples to oranges. Those things were not right, and neither is this!" exclaimed Paul.

##  (E) Emotional Regulation and C (Curiosity)

Wanting to slow the conversation's tempo, Alisha replied, "Let me slow down. No one is saying the solution to ending discrimination is to discriminate. It sounds like you don't think affirmative action is fair because it takes race into consideration and that affirmative action negates taking a student's merits and qualifications into account. Is that correct? I'm interested in your perspective, Paul."

"Yes, that is what I am saying. Why take race into consideration? Race should not be a factor in college admissions. I feel like it is not fair because it undermines the principle of meritocracy by prioritizing race over qualifications and merits. So, if there is a black student and a white student with the same credentials, affirmative action says choose the minority, thus discriminating against the white student. So, the white student is punished for being white, while the black student gets preferential treatment—based on race. That is NOT FAIR!" cried Paul.

"But you're okay with spots being taken by legacy students, athletes, and wealthy families. So, is it fair if a student gets in because their parents donated a significant amount to the school or because they are the legacy to three generations of graduates? No. Where I get frustrated is that, as a society, those preferential practices do not seem to bother anyone. But taking race into account to ensure a diverse student population is a problem," declared Alisha.

"Alisha, I am not saying that any of that is fair. None of it should get you special treatment, including race. I think they should just stick to grades for admission. Alisha, I have known you a long time, and you are one of the smartest people that I know. I guess my question is, why are you so passionate about affirmative action? Why do you think using race as a factor is fair?" asked Paul.

##  R (Respectful Listening at Level 3)

"Paul, I so appreciate you asking me that. From my perspective, it's not an 'either-or'—it's a 'yes, and' situation. I wish things were fair, that merit and qualifications were the basis for college admissions for all students, and that race had no influence on admission. However, history and research have shown us that even when a minority is equally qualified, bias and discrimination creep in, and they are often not chosen, especially in prestigious universities. Paul, my family is not wealthy, and I am a first-generation college graduate who was fortunate enough to graduate from an Ivy league University. Yes, I was valedictorian of my high school class and served as class president. Before affirmative action, there were universities where my merit and exceptional qualifications still would not have mattered because I did not fit the "mold" of their students. I would not have gotten in simply because I am black. But, a white student with fewer credentials could have gotten admitted. How was that fair? Affirmative action was designed to stop those discriminatory practices, combat unconscious bias, and require universities to ensure admission to ALL students who meet all qualifications. It was designed to create more access for minority students, not take it away from white students. I guess, based on my own experiences, this is a very personal topic for me," explained Alisha.

"I did not know that about you, Alisha. I can see how personal this is for you," said Paul sheepishly.

"Honestly, I do not know for sure if I was the beneficiary of affirmative action. But I will tell you, going to an Ivy League school was a dream come true for me and my family. And getting that education is why I am at this job and here with you now. Affirmative action is not the solution to this complex problem because being a minority student is not easy, even with affirmative action. Despite the law, there was still not a lot of diversity, and there were not many people on campus who looked like me. And it creates a stigma. I have had people tell me that the only reason that I was there was because I was a minority. It didn't matter how smart I was, how high my test scores were, or how qualified I was; I constantly felt like I had to prove myself out of the stigma of being an affirmative action student. Even with those experiences, if affirmative action ensured I got a fair shot, I appreciated the opportunity to attend a university that historically was denied to me and wouldn't trade it for anything," said Alicia.

"Wow, Alisha, thank you for sharing that with me. I can see how the concept of affirmative action has personally impacted you. But affirmative action still triggers me to no end because I do not think forcing schools to pick a certain percentage of minority students through racial quotas is going to correct racism. However, I do agree that universities should look at ways to increase student diversity because the world is diverse. But not through the force of affirmative action," said Paul.

"Paul, I agree holding spots for certain groups and racial quotas is not fair in any circumstance, and using racial quotas was banned in the 1970s. The use of race is not a requirement of universities under affirmative action. Universities take a holistic approach to admissions that includes grades, class ranking, test scores, extracurricular activities, letters of recommendation, and essays. Race is often a very small part of the consideration. However, universities could have chosen to consider race as one of many factors for admission to create more diversity in its student population," said Alisha.

"I didn't realize that. I thought that affirmative action forced universities to use racial quotas or decide to admit some students solely based on their race," said Paul.

"No," replied Alisha and continued, "Affirmative action policies worked to eliminate race-based discrimination, not to create them. Universities had to document their admission practices and diversity metrics to ensure fair admission for all. If the university was identified as permitting racial discrimination, it was held accountable, and the practices were declared as unconstitutional. Sadly, it was put in place to try and prevent discrimination and bias. Now, that oversight and those protections no longer exist. Because humans have unconscious bias, I still feel that affirmative action does have a place in

American higher education, but the extent to which it is useful, I agree, is up for debate.

"I still do not believe in affirmative action. I think we should identify a better way to ensure equity and equality at universities. However, I did appreciate this conversation with you and getting a chance to learn more about you. You shared with me many things I never would have been able to consider," said Paul.

"Thank you, Paul. This was helpful for me, too. I often wonder what others think but never take the time to ask. Your concerns are very valid, and I completely understand your perspective. We actually shared a lot of similar beliefs. Like you, it didn't change my mind, but it gave me more to consider around this topic," said Alisha.

Paul and Alisha have successfully navigated a courageous conversation using all the tools of the ACTER model in order. As you will see in the following example, not every conversation will be like that.

## A Courageous Conversation Where Elements of the ACTER Model Bounce Around

"Hey, do I need to go to the website, or can I RSVP with you?" asked Frank.

"I wanted to talk to you about that before you sent your confirmation. We invited Leigh, and I thought you'd want to know," said Jeremy.

Frank took a moment to process what Jeremy said and softened what he originally wanted to say with, "We've been friends since junior high, so why are you inviting my ex-wife to your wedding?" [**Emotional regulation and curiosity**]

"You do remember that Leigh set me and Brice up for our first date, don't you?" asked Jeremy.

The initial shock of knowing he would run into his ex-wife at a wedding reception did obscure that fact. It would be awkward for Jeremy and Brice not to invite Leigh to the wedding. Frank could tell that this wasn't something Jeremy took lightly, nor was it a conversation he wanted to have. Jeremy had a tell when they played poker. He always started rubbing his chin when he was nervous about being dealt a bad set of cards. Given how fast Jeremy's hand was stroking his chin, Frank was surprised his friend hadn't rubbed his beard off. [**Appreciating a diversity of opinion and respectful listening.**]

"Yes, I do remember that. Has she RSVPed yet? Did she get a plus one? Seeing her with a date might be too much for me," said Frank. [**Triggers.**]

"Brice talked to her the other night, and she was on the fence about coming. She had the same reservations about bumping into you, too. Maybe you two could talk and work out something where it's not so awkward. Maybe where neither of you brings a plus one," said Jeremy.

"It means that much to you that Leigh and I are both there? You're willing to jump through all of these hoops to get us both there?" asked Frank. [**Curiosity.**]

"Of course it means a lot to us. You both are part of the reason we're together, and you're an active part of our lives. I wish I knew how to make it less painful for both of you, but I don't," said Jeremy.

"Well, I'll work something out with Leigh because it means so much to you. And I want to be there for you, too," said Frank. [**Appreciation of a diversity of opinion.**]

There's a lot going on in this conversation between Frank and Jeremy. Obviously, this is a conversation that's uncomfortable for both of them. Jeremy has taken a proactive approach to diffuse the powder keg that could have happened had Frank and Leigh run into each other at their wedding. Frank is holding his own, practicing the elements of the ACTER model after being blindsided by the potentially triggering news. Moreover, you can see how Frank and Jeremy's conversation does not follow the ACTER script.

If there is a script to most courageous conversations, it starts precisely like Jeremy and Frank's. Your conversation partner will say something that you aren't prepared to hear. That could be a statement about their political stance on a news article, a personal issue, or any other random bit of information you don't necessarily agree with. It wouldn't be a courageous conversation if that topic were something you wanted to discuss, so you'll need to employ emotional regulation at the beginning of the talk. You won't get too far if the first thing out of your mouth is, "Well, that's the dumbest thing I've ever heard. How could you possibly think that?"

I challenge you to think back to your last few courageous conversations. What was the cadence of the conversation? Can you pinpoint when you could have used one of the elements of the ACTER model? Do your courageous conversations follow any pattern that might make future conversations easier to plan for? Did you practice any of the parts of the ACTER model without knowing you were? If so, how well did you do so?

Asking those types of questions after every courageous conversation is necessary to achieve an overall goal we set at the beginning of this book: "The ACTER model is designed to take the stress out of your side of the conversation to objectively hear your conversation partner's point of view." The key phrase in that statement is "take the stress out of." You can only become more comfortable with any activity by performing and analyzing how you can improve. Think about how nervous you were the first time

197

you drove a car alone. After years and countless miles of driving, I doubt that you think twice about it now.

Driving also gets less stressful when you realize getting to your destination isn't a competition. As I mentioned in the introduction, the ACTER model isn't designed to win debates. You're not in competition with your conversation partner. You're only in competition with yourself. You must struggle with the introspection necessary to identify your triggers and create self-awareness. You will put strategies in place to regulate your emotional response. Every step of the ACTER model requires that you exert control over yourself. It's easy to believe your cause is righteous and battle ideas that differ from yours. After all, conflict with those who are different from us is in our DNA. What's difficult is exercising control over that nature and aligning yourself with trying to understand someone else's point of view. As you utilize the ACTER model, your Emotional Intelligence competencies will increase in the process.

As with any difficult undertaking, there's no shame in asking for help along the way. My colleagues and I stand ready to assist your company or social organization in navigating courageous conversations. If you feel your group would benefit from discussing diversity and inclusion issues, we'd be happy to help you with that, too!

For more information, please visit us at EQStrategists.com.

# Glossary Entries

**The 7-38-55 Rule:** A theory created in the late 1960s by behavioral psychologist Dr. Albert Mehrabian that states all face-to-face communication is 7 percent verbal, 38 percent voice and tone, and 55 percent body language.

**The 80–20 Rule:** A postulate developed by 19th-century economist Vilfredo Federico Damaso Pareto stating that roughly 80 percent of consequences come from 20 percent of causes.

**Active listening:** A communication skill that seeks to gather information about your conversation partner and their beliefs by asking open-ended questions and using other communication techniques.

**Appreciating a diversity of opinion:** The first step in the ACTER model, which seeks to let both parties in a courageous conversation accept differences in the other's point of view.

**Blind spot bias:** Believing that you're less biased than other people.

**Communication mindsets:** Four different ways of approaching a conversation based on your level of competition and defensiveness. The four mindsets are: Win-win, lose-lose, lose-win, and win-lose.

**Courageous conversation:** Any conversation you don't want to have.

**Conversation partner:** The person you're having a discussion with.

**Curiosity:** The second phase of the ACTER model, which holds that when entering conversations and relationships, you assume only that you have something to learn by collecting data about yourself and your conversation partner.

**Divergence of opinions:** Any difference between two or more people's attitudes, opinions, or worldviews. Some typical areas where divergences of opinion can be seen are: political parties, religious preferences, sports teams, or public policies.

**Divergent thinking:** Often called lateral thinking, this is generating multiple creative solutions to the same problem or around the same topic.

**Diversity:** The variation in physical and social characteristics, such as gender, ethnicity, age, and education.

**Emotional intelligence (EI):** The ability to effectively acknowledge, identify, and communicate your emotions, as well as understand the emotions of others.

**Emotional regulation:** The fourth step in the ACTER model, which utilizes the ability or strategies used to exert control over one's emotional state.

**Emotional self-regulation:** The ability to understand the source and extent of your emotions and how the expressions of your emotions affect a courageous conversation.

**Exaggeration:** Adding extraneous nonrelated information in a conversation to prove a point.

**Factors of identity:** External characteristics which are used to categorize people. These can include, but are not limited to, race, gender, religion, ethnicity, sexual orientation, class, or unique abilities.

**Fixed mindset:** A belief that all your traits and beliefs are pre-destined, and there can be little done to change "who you are."

**Gaslighting:** A subtle form of bullying used to sow self-doubt in someone's mind to get the upper hand in a courageous conversation.

**Growth mindset:** A belief that you are always a work in progress and that new experiences and facts help advance your personal development.

**Hyperbolic statements:** Intentional exaggerations to emphasize a point, rather than be taken literally.

**Inclusion:** Procedures that organizations implement to integrate everyone in the group, allowing everyone's differences to coexist in a mutually beneficial way. The goal of inclusion strategies is to make everyone feel accepted and comfortable, ready to share their opinions and thoughts without hesitation.[50]

**Information gap:** A psychological theory that explains curiosity as starting when one sees one's knowledge base is lacking; that gap between knowing and not knowing is the motivation for education.

**Levels of listening:** Three different states of hearing a speaker's message, which include: passionately hearing, listening with a motive, and listening with empathy and curiosity.

**Mental filter:** A cognitive distortion that blocks some stimuli from one's conscious perception while allowing other types of stimuli to be recognized.

**Microaggression:** Common slights or derogatory comments that relate to someone's identity such as: age, gender, sexual orientation, race, body type, or any other defining characteristic.

**Mood elevator:** A theory presented by author Larry Senn in his book, *The Mood Elevator: Take Charge of Your Feelings, Become a Better You.* Senn believes that the quality of your mindset is directly related to your mood.

**Nonverbal cues:** Signals that conversation partners use to communicate intent without speaking.

**Oversimplification:** Omitting critical details in a discussion to prove one's point.

**Pareto principle:** See the 80–20 Rule

**Perceived reality:** A person's subjective experience of events and relationships. When not tempered with self-awareness, a person can believe their perceived reality is the absolute truth when compared with others.

**Perceptual defense:** A selective perception filter blocks information that does not align with your beliefs or preconceived notions.

**Perceptual vigilance:** A selective perception filter that lets you notice information that is significant to you.

**Phrases of appreciation:** Neutral statements given in conversations that show you respect what your conversation partner has to say or that are designed to de-escalate rising tensions during a courageous conversation.

**Phrases of curiosity:** Open-ended questions that you can ask during a conversation that allow your conversation partner to express their thoughts, experiences, and feelings openly and honestly.

**Phrases of emotional triggers/regulation:** Specific questions or statements that are designed to reduce or eliminate the effects of triggers for you or your conversation partner.

**Post-traumatic stress disorder (PTSD):** A psychiatric disorder that can occur in people who have experienced or witnessed a traumatic event, series of events, or set of circumstances.[51]

**Privilege:** A characteristic of a society that assumes social preference or dominance of one group over others. This preference or dominance gives advantage or opportunities that other groups do not have.

**Principles of engagement:** Different methods of communication that can include informing, consulting, involving, collaborating, or empowering.

**Respectful listening:** The fifth and final phase of the ACTER model seeks for both parties to go beyond active listening techniques and search for meaning in nonverbal communication elements such as: timing, speed of speech, body language, and cultural/historical contexts.

**Selective perception:** The process whereby individuals perceive the information they want to hear while ignoring opposing viewpoints.

**Separate realities:** The psychological theory that no two individuals have the same experience of any given event.

**Snap judgment:** Assessing a situation based on a single data point.

**Trauma:** The result of experiences that leave one feeling unsafe and often helpless.[52]

**Triggers:** The third phase of the ACTER model. This step looks to limit or manage topics, phrases, events, or circumstances that produce an uncomfortable emotional response, such as anxiety, frustration, panic, or discomfort during a courageous conversation.

**Verbal abuse:** A type of abuse that uses writing or speech to bully, intimidate, scold, or otherwise demean someone's self-esteem.

# Bibliography

Ackerman, Courtney E. "87 Self-Reflection Questions for Introspection [+Exercises]." Positive Psychology, December 18, 2017. https://positivepsychology.com/introspection-self-reflection/.

Adams, Shona. "Are Cognitive Distortions Much More Important than You Realised?" Research Gate, May 12, 2019. https://www.researchgate.net/publication/333032817_Are_cognitive_distortions_much_more_important_than_you_realised.

American Psychiatric Association. "What Is Posttraumatic Stress Disorder (PTSD)?" What is Posttraumatic Stress Disorder (PTSD)? Accessed December 5, 2022. https://www.psychiatry.org/patients-families/ptsd/what-is-ptsd.

Andželika. "26 Email Phrases That Seem Polite, but Actually Have a Different Meaning." Bored Panda, July 8, 2022. https://www.boredpanda.com/passive-aggressive-email-phrases-meaning/?utm_source=google&utm_medium=organic&utm_campaign=organic.

Angelo, Megan. "16 Unforgettable Things Maya Angelou Wrote and Said." Glamour, May 28, 2014. https://www.glamour.com/story/maya-angelou-quotes.

Atske, Sara. "Americans and 'Cancel Culture': Where Some See Calls for Accountability, Others See Censorship, Punishment." Pew Research Center: Internet, Science & Tech, June 30, 2022. https://www.pewresearch.org/internet/2021/05/19/americans-and-cancel-culture-where-some-see-calls-for-accountability-others-see-censorship-punishment/.

Beohm, Rachel. "5 Signs You're Making Someone Uncomfortable." Rachel Beohm | Writer, Speaker, Coach, March 22, 2022. https://www.rachelbeohm.com/5-signs-of-discomfort/.

Breindel, Alexander. "20 Signs You're an Overly Judgmental Person." Best Life, October 31, 2018. https://bestlifeonline.com/overly-judgmental-signs/.

Brown, Brené. Atlas of the Heart. London: Vermilion, 2021.

Brownlee, Dana. "Dear White People: When You Say You 'Don't See Color,' This Is What We Really Hear." Forbes Magazine, July 6, 2022. https://www.forbes.com/sites/danabrownlee/2022/06/19/dear-white-people-when-you-say-you-dont-see-color-this-is-what-we-really-hear/?sh=55a9acb326d6.

Brueck, Hilary. "The Best Time of Day to Do Everything at Work, According to Science." Business Insider, August 13, 2018. https://tinyurl.com/35d3e99h.

Buxton, Scott. "Make Courageous Conversations Your Secret Weapon." Physiospot, October 12, 2022. https://www.physiospot.com/2021/08/18/make-courageous-conversations-your-secret-weapon/.

Cameron, C. Daryl, Cendri A. Hutcheson, Amanda M. Ferguson, Julian A. Scheffer, Eliana Hadjiandreou, and Michael Inzlicht. "Empathy Is Hard Work: People Choose to Avoid Empathy Because of Its Cognitive Costs." *Journal of Experimental Psychology.* General. U.S. National Library of Medicine, June 2019. https://pubmed.ncbi.nlm.nih.gov/30998038/.

Cantril, Hadley, and Albert H. Hastorf. "They Saw a Game; A Case Study." *American Psychological Association*, 1951. https://psycnet.apa.org/record/1954-07342-001.

Centers for Disease Control and Prevention. "Radon and Your Health." Radon and Your Health. Centers for Disease Control and Prevention, January 3, 2022. https://www.cdc.gov/nceh/features/protect-home-radon/index.html.

Cherry, Kendra. "What Is Revenge Bedtime Procrastination?" Verywell Mind, March 1, 2023. https://www.verywellmind.com/what-is-revenge-bedtime-procrastination-5189591.

Chew, Stephen L. "Myth: Eyewitness Testimony Is the Best Kind of Evidence." Association for Psychological Science, August 20, 2018. https://www.psychologicalscience.org/teaching/myth-eyewitness-testimony-is-the-best-kind-of-evidence.html.

Christensen, Tricia. "In Baseball, What Is a Batting Average?" Sports & Hobbies, September 3, 2022. https://www.sportsnhobbies.org/in-baseball-what-is-a-batting-average.htm.

Cline, Austin. "What Are Oversimplification and Exaggeration Fallacies?" ThoughtCo, May 29, 2021. https://www.thoughtco.com/oversimplification-and-exaggeration-fallacies-3968441.

Coursera. "What Is Effective Communication? Skills for Work, School, and Life." Coursera, April 14, 2023. https://www.coursera.org/articles/communication-effectiveness.

Day One. "What Is Verbal Abuse?" Day One Crisis Hotline. Accessed April 12, 2023. http://dayoneservices.org/verbal-abuse/.

Dweck, Carol S. *Mindset*. London: Robinson, 2017.

Exploring Your Mind. "The Invisible Gorilla: A Classic Experiment in Perception." Exploring Your Mind, June 2, 2020. https://exploringyourmind.com/the-invisible-gorilla-a-classic-experiment-in-perception.

Feinberg School of Medicine. "Principles of Engagement." Center for Community Health. Feinberg School of Medicine: Northwestern University. Accessed November 4, 2022. https://www.feinberg.northwestern.edu/sites/cch/about/principles-of-engagement.html.

# Bibliography

Forbes, Sophie. "18 Gestures That Can Cause Offense around the World." ShermansTravel, February 4, 2020. https://www.shermanstravel.com/advice/18-gestures-that-can-cause-offense-around-the-world.

Franklin, Benjamin. " Forbes Quotes: Thoughts on the Business of Life." Forbes Magazine. Accessed May 16, 2023. https://www.forbes.com/quotes/1116/.

Gellman, Marc. "How We See Sharon--and Israel." Newsweek. Newsweek, March 13, 2010. https://www.newsweek.com/how-we-see-sharon-and-israel-108309.

George, Kaylene. "How to Recognize You're Triggered in 4 Simple Steps." Advocacy & Accommodations, Autistic Behaviors, February 11, 2020. https://autisticmama.com/recognize-youre-triggered/.

Goleman, Daniel. "What Is Emotional Self-Awareness?" Korn Ferry, April 2, 2021. https://www.korn-ferry.com/insights/this-week-in-leadership/what-is-emotional-self-awareness.

Grande, Diane. "Active Listening Skills." Psychology Today, June 2, 2020. https://www.psychologytoday.com/us/blog/in-it-together/202006/active-listening-skills.

Grivas, Theodoros B, and Olga D Savvidou. "Melatonin the 'Light of Night' In Human Biology and Adolescent Idiopathic Scoliosis." National Library of Medicine, April 4, 2007. https://www.ncbi.nlm.nih.gov/pmc/articles/PMC1855314/.

Hamer, Ashley. "Here's Why Smells Trigger Such Vivid Memories." Discovery, August 1, 2019. https://tinyurl.com/mrx6shnt.

Harvard Health. "Understanding the Stress Response." Harvard Medical School, July 6, 2020. https://www.health.harvard.edu/staying-healthy/understanding-the-stress-response.

Hill, Ross. "We Need to Stop Misusing the Word 'Triggered'." The Mighty, April 23, 2020. https://themighty.com/topic/mental-health/stop-misusing-triggered-mental-health/.

Hillard, Scott. "10 Common Human Behaviors Explained with Science." Listverse, June 21, 2014. https://listverse.com/2013/07/11/10-human-actions-with-biological-explanations-2/.

Hogue, Tiffany. "Managing Judgement in a Judgemental World." High Country Behavioral Health, February 2, 2021. https://tinyurl.com/4cvn34zd.

Homeless Resource Network. "Factors Contributing to Homelessness." Homeless Resource Network, June 12, 2012. https://homelessresourcenetwork.org/?page_id=1086.

Houghton, Emily. "Levels of Listening." The People Piece, November 17, 2020. https://www.peoplepiece.com/our-insights/levels-of-listening.

# Bibliography

Howard, Jacqueline. "'Eavesdropping' Study Yields Huge
Surprise About Human Awareness." HuffPost, June 21,
2012. https://tinyurl.com/4v95j4u4.

Kafi, Yashar. "The Growth vs. Fixed Mindset." Amplify
Resources Strategic Consulting. Accessed June 5, 2022.
https://tinyurl.com/yck3dudb.

Kerr, James. "What Is Your Company's Human Operating System?"
Inc.com, December 5, 2016. https://tinyurl.com/m8zz5mus.

Kruse, Kevin. "The 80/20 Rule and How It Can
Change Your Life." *Forbes Magazine*, October
12, 2022. https://www.forbes.com/sites/
kevinkruse/2016/03/07/80-20-rule/?sh=6011fe653814.

Lee, Kristen. "Why Is It so Hard to Set Boundaries?"
*Psychology Today*. Sussex Publishers, September
11, 2018. https://www.psychologytoday.com/us/
blog/rethink-your-way-the-good-life/201809/
why-is-it-so-hard-set-boundaries.

Lombrozo, Tania. "Is Curiosity a Positive or Negative
Feeling?" NPR, September 25, 2017. https://www.
npr.org/sections/13.7/2017/09/25/553443078/
is-curiosity-a-positive-or-negative-feeling.

Lyford, Chris. "The Trigger Warning Controversy."
Psychotherapy Networker. Accessed November 27,
2022. https://www.psychotherapynetworker.org/blog/
details/1057/the-trigger-warning-controversy.

Marinaki, Alexandra. "Diversity vs. Inclusion in the Workplace." Recruiting Resources: How to Recruit and Hire Better, August 11, 2022. https://tinyurl.com/5cjc9czw.

McCombs School of Business. "Working Together Is Easier If You Can Distinguish Perspective-Taking from Empathy." University of Texas at Austin Research Showcase, January 9, 2019. https://research.utexas.edu/showcase/articles/view/working-together-is-easier-if-you-can-distinguish-perspective-taking-from-empathy.

McGowan, Kat. "Learning Not to Lash Out." Psychology Today, September 1, 2005. https://www.psychologytoday.com/us/articles/200509/learning-not-lash-out.

Michail, Jon. "Council Post: Strong Nonverbal Skills Matter Now More than Ever in This 'New Normal.'" Forbes, October 12, 2022. https://www.forbes.com/sites/forbescoaches-council/2020/08/24/strong-nonverbal-skills-matter-now-more-than-ever-in-this-new-normal/?sh=55189f675c61.

Oppong, Thomas. "To Think Clearly, You Must Actively Overcome Your Blind Spots." Medium, April 19, 2021. https://medium.com/personal-growth/to-think-cle-arly-you-must-actively-overcome-your-blind-spots-c2a43c34657d.

Palmer, David A. "Human Operating Systems." Medium. The New Mindscape, September 1, 2021. https://medium.com/the-new-mindscape/human-operating-systems-871a13993c26.

Paul Ekman Group. "Universal Emotions." Paul Ekman Group, November 5, 2022. https://www.paulekman.com/universal-emotions/.

Pinsker, Joe. "Do People Crave Foods Their Moms Ate during Pregnancy?" *The Atlantic*, February 4, 2020. https://tinyurl.com/4tpx24kx.

Plata , Mariana. "How to Spot Your Emotional Triggers." Psychology Today. Sussex Publishers, October 31, 2018. https://www.psychologytoday.com/us/blog/the-gen-y-psy/201810/how-spot-your-emotional-triggers.

Plata, Mariana. "6 Ways to Practice Self-Curiosity |." Psychology Today, January 10, 2020. https://www.psychologytoday.com/us/blog/the-gen-y-psy/202001/6-ways-practice-self-curiosity.

Portes, Dan. "Selective Perception and Leadership." Management Resource Group, December 7, 2021. https://www.mrgpeople.com/blog/selective-perception.

Rabikrisson, Arthi. "Council Post: Practice New Habits to Eliminate Blind Spot Bias." *Forbes Magazine*, May 27, 2021. https://www.forbes.com/sites/forbescoachescouncil/2021/05/27/practice-new-habits-to-eliminate-blind-spot-bias/?sh=128876857b44.

Raypole, Crystal. "Emotional Triggers: Defintion and How to Manage Them." Healthline, November 13, 2020. https://www.healthline.com/health/mental-health/emotional-triggers.

Resnick, Ariane. "How to Deal with Verbal Abuse." Verywell Mind, February 16, 2023. https://www.verywellmind.com/how-to-deal-with-verbal-abuse-5205616.

Richo, David. "13 Strategies to Deal with Your Emotional Triggers." Experience Life, July 22, 2022. https://experiencelife.lifetime.life/article/13-strategies-to-deal-with-your-emotional-triggers/.

Sarkis, Stephanie. "11 Red Flags of Gaslighting in a Relationship." Psychology Today, January 22, 2017. https://www.psychologytoday.com/us/blog/here-there-and-everywhere/201701/11-red-flags-of-gaslighting-in-a-relationship.

Sasson, Remez. "What Is Curiosity and Why It Is Important." Success Consciousness , October 3, 2022. https://www.successconsciousness.com/blog/personal-development/what-is-curiosity/.

Scheffer, Julian A., C. Daryl Cameron, and Michael Inzlicht. "Caring Is Costly: People Avoid the Cognitive Work of Compassion." *Journal of Experimental Psychology*. General. U.S. National Library of Medicine, August 19, 2021. https://pubmed.ncbi.nlm.nih.gov/34410802/.

Senn, Larry E. *The Mood Elevator: Take Charge of Your Feelings, Become a Better You.* Oakland, CA: Berrett-Koehler Publishers, Inc., 2017.

# Bibliography

Simons, Llana. "Why Do We Have Emotions?" Psychology Today, November 14, 2009. https://www.psychologytoday.com/us/blog/the-literary-mind/200911/why-do-we-have-emotions.

Smith, Jennifer. "Growth Mindset vs Fixed Mindset: How What You Think Affects What You Achieve." Mindset Health, September 25, 2020. https://www.mindsethealth.com/matter/growth-vs-fixed.

Steinhilber, Brianna. "5 Signs Someone's Lying to You." NBCNews.com, August 15, 2017. https://www.nbcnews.com/better/health/how-tell-if-someone-lying-according-behavioral-experts-ncna786326.

Stromberg, Joseph. "The Real Reason American Public Transportation Is Such a Disaster." Vox, August 10, 2015. https://www.vox.com/2015/8/10/9118199/public-transportation-subway-buses.

Suttie, Jill. "Why Curious People Have Better Relationships." Greater Good, May 21, 2017. https://greatergood.berkeley.edu/article/item/why_curious_people_have_better_relationships.

Taft, Tiffany, ed. "Intent vs Impact: Meaning, Examples, & Which Matters More." Healthline, April 28, 2021. https://www.healthline.com/health/intent-vs-impact#which-is-more-important.

The Jed Foundation. "Understanding Emotional Trauma: Jed." The Jed Foundation, May 11, 2022. https://jedfoundation. org/resource/understanding-emotional-trauma/.

United States Department of Veterans Affairs. How Common is PTSD in Veterans?, July 24, 2018. https://www.ptsd. va.gov/understand/common/common_veterans.asp.

University of Western Alabama. "The Science of Emotion: Exploring the Basics of Emotional Psychology." UWA Online, June 22, 2020. https://online.uwa.edu/news/ emotional-psychology/.

Valenti, Zach. *The Dirty Little Secret about Growth Mindset. YouTube*, 2016. https://youtu.be/zionUl13Dko.

Viki, Tendayi. "Why Diverse Teams Are More Creative." *Forbes Magazine*, December 8, 2016. https:// www.forbes.com/sites/tendayiviki/2016/12/06/ why-diverse-teams-are-more-creative/?sh=3f8ba99e7262.

Vogel, Kaitlin. "7 Manipulation Tactics to Know." Psych Central, April 15, 2022. https://psychcentral.com/lib/tactics-ma- nipulators-use-to-win-and-confuse-you#spotting-ma- nipulation.

Whistler, Adam. "The 22 Worst Tech Predictions of All Time." Hero Labs, December 3, 2019. https://www.hero-labs.com/ stories/the-22-worst-tech-predictions-of-all-time/.

Yarow, Jay. "Here's What Steve Ballmer Thought about the iPhone Five Years Ago." Business Insider, June 29, 2012. https://www.businessinsider.com/heres-what-steve-ballmer-thought-about-the-iphone-five-years-ago-2012-6.

Zalis, Shelley. "The Truth about Diversity—and Why It Matters." *Forbes Magazine*, December 6, 2017. https://www.forbes.com/sites/shelleyzalis/2017/11/30/the-truth-about-diversity-and-why-it-matters/?sh=da441e466e71.

Zojceska, Anja. "Top 10 Benefits of Diversity in the Workplace." Blog, January 24, 2022. https://www.talentlyft.com/en/blog/article/244/top-10-benefits-of-diversity-in-the-workplace.

# Endnotes

1 Coursera, 2023.

2 Buxton, 2022.

3 Dweck, 2017.

4 Atske, 2021.

5 Zalis, 2017.

6 Viki, 2016.

7 Zojceska, 2022.

8 Howard, 2012.

9 Exploring Your Mind, 2020.

10 Exploring Your Mind, 2020.

11 Howard, 2012.

12 Gellman, 2010.

13 Chew, 2018.

14 Cantril, Hadley, and Albert H. Hastorf, 1951.

15 Rabikrisson, 2021.

16 Brownlee, 2022.

17 Oppong, 2021.

18 Sasson, 2022.

19 Suttie, 2017.

20 Lombrozo, 2017

21 Yarow, 2012.

22 Yarow, 2012.

23 Whistler, 2019.

24 Whistler, 2019.

25 Whistler, 2019.

26 Hogue, 2021.

27 This quote is generally attributed to Tumblr user nikolae-cuza. But, as with most meme wisdom, it's difficult to definitively pin down a precise source.

28 Christensen, 2022.

29 Brown, 2022.

30 Hamer, 2019.

31 The Jed Foundation, 2022.

32 The National Mental Health Alliance (https://www.nami.org/Home) is a great resource for finding assistance with any mental health issues. Also, don't forget that many health insurance plans include counseling options that aren't advertised with copays and deductibles. Some companies also have counseling benefits outside of normal health insurance, so check with your human resources department to see if assistance is available.

33 American Psychiatric Association, 2022.

34 United States Department of Veterans Affairs, 2018.

35 Harvard Health, 2022.

36 Franlin, 2023.

37 Kruse, 2016.

38 There's tons of great research out there on examples of the 80–20 Rule that far exceeds the scope of this book. If you're interested in the topic and how to apply the principle to your life, I strongly suggest checking out *The 80/20 Principle: The Secret of Achieving More with Less* by Richard Koch.

39 Beohm, 2022.

40 Adams, 2019.

41 Homeless Resource Network, 2012.

42 Paul Ekman Group, 2022. During the 1970s, psychologist Paul Eckman suggested that six basic emotions were universally experienced in all human cultures. Eckman's list is as good as any for our purposes here.

43 University of Western Alabama, 2020.

44 Michail, 2020.

45  Brueck, 2018.

46 Steinhilber, 2017. A quick note that eye contact avoidance in Western cultures has never been proven to mean deceit. Experts in this article say that deviation from baseline behaviors are more indicative of deception than breaking eye contact.

47 Angelo, 2014.

48 Day One, 2023.

49 Resnick, 2023. Thanks to Ariane Resnick for her article on dealing with the little talked about topic of verbal abuse. If you can't call either of the resources listed in the text, visit Day One's website at: http://dayoneservices.org/verbal-abuse or That's Not Cool's website at: https://thatsnotcool.com/stop-verbal-abuse-online-get-help.

50 Marinaki, 2022.

51 American Psychiatric Association, 2022.

52 The Jed Foundation, 2022.

Made in United States
North Haven, CT
21 January 2025